My Summer Vacation:
The Victorio Campaign Journal of Robert Grierson
1880

Lawrence John Francell

Purple Feather Press
Georgetown, TX 78628
www.PurpleFeatherPress.com

Table of Contents

Illustrations

Table of Contents

Illustrations

Map of the Area of Operations in West Texas

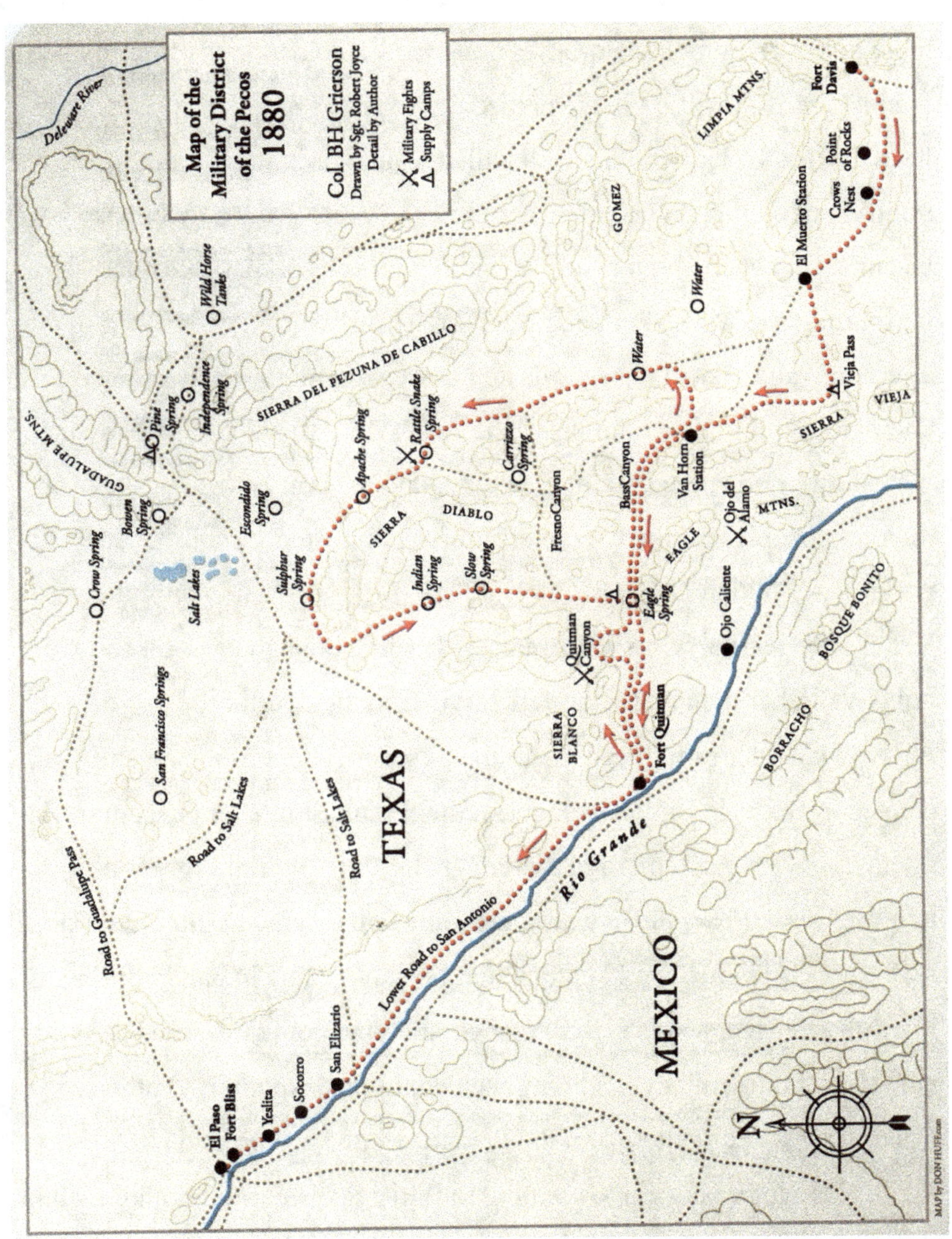

Introduction

Some of my fondest memories came from sitting at the kitchen table in my grandmother-in-law's house as she told stories of family and the history of the little village named after the old Army post, Fort Davis. Lucy Foster Miller, whom we all called Daughter in the Southern tradition of a child named after her mother, would brew coffee, bake biscuits, fry bacon and tell stories without missing a beat. Weather permitting, she worked in her garden in the early morning, dressed in the afternoon, and visited her friends and those who might be ill and need company. Within the community she was "Miss Lucy." She fed anyone who showed up at the door at mealtime, and the house was always open to young people and lively conversation on almost any subject, especially politics. A lifelong Democrat, she did not own a television until the Watergate Hearings. In 1967 I married her granddaughter Beth, and we now live in her home near the Jeff Davis County Courthouse.

Daughter introduced me to the Superintendent of the recently created Fort Davis National Historic Site, Frank Smith, and encouraged me to apply for a summer job there, which I did. I worked for Frank for two summers, 1967-68. He was a demon when it came to interpretation, a skill I hope I learned well and one that certainly came in handy during a forty year museum career. Frank taught that one not just learned the story but knew it intrinsically, and only then could one explain it to others. Frank's ashes are scattered on the Parade Ground at Fort Davis.

Daughter also introduced me to Barry Scobee. I did not know him well, but one day after he and I met, she dispatched me over to his house to collect some photographs that she had decided he needed to donate to the historic site. That was the only time I had a personal visit. However, everyone knew Barry. He arrived in the mountains as the assistant to Carlysle Graham Rath, who was doing research for his book, *The Romance of the Davis Mountains and Big Bend*, originally published in 1919. Over the years Scobee wrote three histories of Fort Davis. The first was a pamphlet written in 1936 during the Texas Centennial, and created for the WPA Writers' Project. The second, in 1947, was mostly a repeat of Rath's *Romance* but concentrated on Fort Davis. Finally, in 1963 he wrote his third book and was able to break into the realm of actual history and move away from the legends and folk tales that haunted the region. Regardless, Scobee would be the first to say that he was a newspaper man and not an historian.

Born in Missouri on May 2, 1885, Scobee alternated between newspaper work and stints in the army both in the Philippines and World War I. He and his wife Kathleen finally settled permanently at Fort Davis in 1925. He served as Jeff Davis County Justice of the Peace, but primarily made a living as a "stringer" for a variety of newspapers. At the time the Fort Worth *Star-Telegram* and San Angelo *Standard-Times* covered the region, due in part to stories submitted by Scobee. Incongurously, Scobee also wrote short stories for a variety of what were known as popular or pulp magazines. A founding member of the Fort Davis Historical Society, Scobee was instrumental in the creation of the Fort Davis National Historic Site, a unit of the National Park Service. The Society, organized in 1953, took on the mission of saving the old army post.

Recognized as the premier local historian Scobee was one of the leaders in the effort that proved successful on July 4, 1963, when the National Park service took over the old Army post. In the meantime he became the depository or many of the documents related to the history of the area. One of those documents was the Victorio Campaign journal of Robert Grierson, the acquisition of which is better told by Scobee himself.

The names most often associated with the Indian Wars are George Armstrong Custer, Nelson Miles, George Crook and, on the other side, Geronimo, Crazy Horse, and Sitting Bull. However, two others deserve their place in the pantheon of names of the period. The Warm Springs Apache Victorio led the Army on a merry chase through southern New Mexico and West Texas for years, and his adversary in Texas, Colonel Benjamin Henry Grierson, the Colonel of the 10th United States Cavalry, would eventually run him to ground.

The Victorio Campaign in Texas suffered from a lack of public press. While reporters from the East fawned over Custer and his exploits, and the pursuit of Geronimo by George Crook and then Nelson Miles were covered extensively, no reporters found themselves in the isolated and rugged Chihuahuan Desert of West Texas. Luckily, there was one person along who did document the campaign, and who was certainly as articulate and observant as any newspaper reporter would have been. Robert Grierson, the colonel's son, was also closer to the action and the decision-making process than any outside observer. However, while known to historians, Robert's journal has never been published in full. It is a firsthand account by an intelligent young man. He is obviously biased and protective of his father, but he, nonetheless, presents the facts, sometimes with a sense of humor and always with a sense of awe.

Robert spoke German, was reading Jules Verne's *Around the World in Eighty Days* in the original French, and was studying Spanish during the campaign. He loved the ladies, particularly the girls he left behind in Jacksonville, Illinois, and constantly fretted over the arrival of the mail that might include letters. He carried the photographs of several of these young women and was always eager to show them to his traveling companions. During his school days in Illinois, virtually unsupervised while his parents were stationed at Fort Concho, the mothers of Jacksonville considered him a menace, but he assured his mother that he was a "good boy."

Robert was respectful of the soldiers and officers of the regiment, demonstrating little of the racial prejudice of the day, an example set by his father. He was protective of his father, "Papa," and quick to defend the colonel at real or perceived slight. He was articulate, observant, and possessed of a keen sense of humor. He was anxious to fit in and worried about how he would react if there was a fight. He made himself a part of his father's headquarters staff, assisting in copying reports and orders. He readily shared the hardships of life in the field and left one of the most interesting first-hand accounts of that long-fought and hard campaign.

Juxtaposed to his father's official report of the campaign, written in calm, matter-of-fact military language, Robert's journal provides a sense of high adventure and wonder. A keen observer, he presents interesting descriptions of many of the personalities involved, especially those who would criticize his father or did not perform in a manner

Robert thought appropriate. His descriptions of the country and the difficulties of travel through the desert region covered in the campaign are detailed and accurate. If one has the desire to understand the landscape traversed by Victorio and his pursuers, one should drive State Highway 54 along the east side of the Sierra Diablo Mountains from Van Horn to Guadalupe Mountains National Park.

The campaign against Victorio is especially well covered in a variety of books listed in the footnotes and bibliography. In retelling his story I have tried to use Grierson's own words as much as possible as a contrast to Robert's writing of the same events. The colonel is precise, objective, and military. Robert writes like a young man out for adventure, who, as his father said, "suddenly found it."

In 1880 the United States Army was midway between two wars, the Civil War and the Spanish-American War. With no thought of conflict with a European nation on the horizon, the small Regular Army functioned more as a constabulary to keep the peace on the large western frontier. At the same time the massive surplus materials left over from the Civil War were running out. In that year's report the Quartermaster-General complained that no Congressional appropriation had been made for new clothing and equipage and that "the difficulties and embarrassments continue, and have increased as the stock of old war clothing has gradually become exhausted."[1] As a consequence of these issues, the military leadership was slowly attempting changes that conformed to the realities of protecting the frontier.

---

[1] *Annual Report of the Secretary of War for the Year 1889* (Washington: Government Printing Office, 1880) p. xii. (Google Books)

Departments and districts were slowly being realigned to conform to strategic requirements. The protection of the railroads throughout the frontier became a primary mission, particularly as the Army served as rapid-response system for the movement of troops to locations of need. The constant movement of troops from post to post prompted the request from both the Quartermaster-General and the Commissary-General that permanent personnel be assigned to these duties at each fort. At the time line officers were assigned to these duties subject to the vagaries of frontier service, and the ensuing disorganization was often inevitable. The Commissary-General also requested the creation of cooking schools and the specific recruitment of cooks and bakers, as opposed to the normal procedure of assigning men from the ranks. In another important organizational move, the Chief of Engineers assigned officers to the various field commands to produce adequate and up-to-date maps.

The total expense for the Army for the year 1880 was $40,000,000. To put that in perspective, by 1864 the Civil War was costing the national treasury $2,000,000 per day.[2] In 1880 the Army consisted of eleven general officers, 1,989 officers, and 24,214 enlisted personnel for the line. Included were an additional 555 officers and 1,286 enlisted personnel in staff positions. However, due to illness, detached duty and desertion the effective force for actual duty was closer to 24,000. As a consequence, in each annual appropriation request there was a call for more personnel. According to the Secretary of War's 1880 *Report,* "The General and Lieutenant-General of the Army concur in the opinion

---

[2] Joseph Wheelan, *Bloody Spring: Forty Days that Sealed the Confederacy's Fate* (Boston: DaCapo Press, 2014), p. 23.

that the Army is too small in enlisted men to fulfill the heavy duties now imposed on it, and that it is overworked."[3] No relief from Congress was forthcoming. However, to Colonel Grierson and the men of the 10th Cavalry actively engaging Victorio in the desert of West Texas these were matters of little consequence.

As with any other occupation historians learn their trade somewhere. I was lucky enough to have two special mentors, both now gone. Dr. Edward Phillips at Austin College thought tests were for the intellectually lazy and made us research and write, and then research and write some more. We stayed friends, and one of my best days was when Ed and I explored Fort Davis National Historic site top to bottom. Dr. Jack Sunder, my graduate advisor at the University of Texas at Austin, also believed that an historian read voraciously, researched thoroughly and wrote clearly. My goal is to make them proud, and any misses on my part are not their fault, but rather my inattention in class.

Help also comes from many quarters. The staff at Fort Davis National Historic Site was invaluable, especially the assistance of John Heiner, Chief of Interpretation, and Bill Manhart, Education and Volunteer Coordinator. I now have a wonderful, long-distance relationship with Hillary Peppers, Adult Services Librarian, at the Jacksonville, Illinois, Public Library. I kept asking questions, and she kept providing answers, all in good humor.

Dr. Michael Powell, Emeritus Professor of Biology and Director of the Herbarium at Sul Ross State University, Alpine, Texas, is the expert in plants of the Big Bend and West Texas. Mike's wife Shirley, a

---

[3] *Annual Report,* p. v.

good friend to have, was often the interlocutor in the many email exchanges. He provided a wealth of information about the plants Robert described in his journal. Kelly Bryan, retired Texas Parks & Wildlife Naturalist, provided information about birds, especially on the question of whether or not roadrunners, not a known food source, were edible. As Robert drew close to El Paso, I was able to rely on the expertise of Bernie Sargent, Regional Historian, for his expertise on all things related to El Paso.

Dr. Beverly Six, retired Professor of English at Sul Ross State University, read the manuscript with a critical eye that was deeply appreciated. She made it better, although errors of fact are still mine.

Finally there is the question, "where is Robert's original journal?" When Barry Scobee died many of his papers found their way into the hands of a local ranch woman. In this world there are always those people who think that they own history by the mere possession of documents, which they feel disinclined to share. She is gone now, and the massive amount of historical material she possessed is now in the hands of heirs. They either feel disinclined to share, or more likely, they do not know what they have. My hope is that someday someone in the family will go through all this material and realize that history belongs to all of us.

We live in Daughter's home, and my office is in the old bathhouse dating from the days before indoor plumbing was installed. On many days, but still too few or this book would have been done much sooner, I disappear into my office, and to her credit Beth assumes I am actually working. She has been my greatest support in this endeavor, even when I have not been there to assist with her first love, her garden.

Barry Scobee's Introduction to the Journal of Robert Grierson

The manner in which Robert Grierson's Victorio War Journal came into my possession is indeed remarkable, out of this world, chance, luck or what have you. With no credit to me for its preservation.

A great deal could be told of Robert's few years at Fort Davis, but this bit of writing exclusively concerns the Journal, which can be called the history of the Victorio campaign, or the Revelation of the thinking of an intelligent young man.

In 1885 Harry Grierson, one of Robert's two brothers who lived out their years at Fort Davis, bought from George Brenner, a native of Germany and bandmaster of the Tenth Cavalry, a two story, roomy house a mile or so east of the Army Post. Harry and his brother lived there for a long time. It was long referred to as the Old Grierson Homestead, supposedly meaning where the General and Mrs. Grierson lived. This is largely wrong. It never was home and hearth of the senior Grierson's. The General owned here only a small tract of land down-canyon on the road to Alpine. His step-son, Harold King, inherited that by bequest.

But Robert, older, acquired land before Harry did. On September 15, 1883, he bought acreage from an El Paso man, Michael Ash. He named it Spring Valley. It lies at the northeast edge of town. It is probable that the senior Grierson's visited there. My correspondence with the latter Grierson's is decidedly skimpy about "Uncle Ben" at Fort Davis.

That in this period life was happy to Bob and his brothers, and busy, is revealed by countless pages of diaries written by Robert. He wrote daily. Much of it is extant today. The "diaries" should not be confused with the Journal. The diaries told of the three brother's activities, and events, and this and that. Robert speaks in them of trying to teach Harry mathematics so that he could qualify to West Point. Robert was mentally, intellectually brilliant, far above the average, apparently. The Journal presents something of this.

Then in 1888 Robert was elected Jeff Davis County commissioner. About that time the county treasurer absconded with the public funds. Robert and another well known citizen were on his office bond. The other commissioners demanded that the bondsmen make good. So Robert and S.A. Townsend had to fork up, their loss being about $2000. The affair hit Robert hard, not so much the money side, likely, as the meanness, the crime, the shame of the thing. This blow fell in November 1889. Two months later the court minutes recorded that Commissioner Grierson was physically incapacitated and absent from the state due to circumstances beyond his control. Thus ended the brilliant Robert's days in Fort Davis.

The following 30 to 40 years of Grierson history is largely a blank to me. In 1917 my pal/wife Katherine and I left my military reporting job on the San Antonio *Express* to come to Fort Davis and work with Carlysle Graham Rath in gathering material for an area history book he planned to write, and did, and saw it published in 1919.

Soon after my arrival Carl set out one day to interview George and Harry Grierson, to acquire a lot of history on the famous family. He had to ask a neighbor where the brothers lived. This was because Harry and George were physically and mentally ambulatory, living first in one house, than another, without explanation, and sometimes singly and alone.

On this pleasant day Carl drove to a house that is now the home of my friend Cecilio Chacon, within calling distance from my home where I am writing this, which is locally known as "Scobee's Shack." Carl knocked at the front door, then, no response, he went around the house, leaving me alone in his cut-down, one seat, red Buick, where I sat fascinatedly watching three buzzards floating high in the sunny June sky. I being thrilled because I thought in my city ignorance that they were mighty winged eagles.

In a couple of minutes Carl came back with a tight, set look on his face. He drove away without a word, looking as if – to use an old saying – he could bite a nail in two. It was several years before I comprehended that hard expression on Carl's mug. By that time I had learned that the Grierson brothers could be polite, courteous – Harry could be princely – and quite otherwise if one asked too many questions about the family history – and don't I know!

Gradually I became casually acquainted with George and Harry. In 1934 Harry took to his sickbed at the Big House. I heard that men were at his side day and night. Meeting three of them together I offered to take turns at the bedside. They gave me a sort of startled, suspicious stare, and walked away. In a day or so word came, flatly, that they did not need me. It was a flat rebuff, but I was not offended, knowing how they might feel about a "newcomer," an outsider, a man who did not belong edging into their lifetime acquaintance with the noted Grierson's.

Harry died in an El Paso hospital July 13, 1934, and was buried at the Grierson family's old home town of Jacksonville, Ill. Not a great while afterward George developed a disposition that made it advisable for him to go away to an institution. With George gone, the county judge had, under the law, to name a guardian of the estate. Judge Edwin H. Fowlkes appointed T.M. (Mead) Wilson, the Grierson family banker in Marfa; and three appraisers of the property to set values. The three were Bob Mulhern, son of a famous, old-time, long gone Army ordnance sergeant; Harold Thompson, son of one of the men who had to make good on the absconding treasurer's bond; and one who didn't belong, Barry Scobee. Mrs. Wilson came in as our clerical recorder with her clip board and pencil.

Every item in the Big House was listed, upstairs and down. I told at the time, and so remember now, that on the floor of the large front, or living, room were seven large wooden boxes, the size of old-fashioned trunks, with lids like trunks.

I raised the lid of one and saw that the box was full of books. I took up one, then two more, and saw that they had fine, steel engravings for the illustrations. I tried another box, and thumbed at four or five volumes, and found that the flyleaves and other pages had rubber stamp imprints, or inked or penciled names of army post and fort libraries from evidently all over the U.S. Years later a Grierson kinswoman who inherited all her cousin's property by will gave me a leather-back book, a Bible of all things, from a soldiers' library – that has on the flyleaf a book sticker with the printed words, "library of the Tenth Infantry, '77; then under it, handwriting in ink, "by Mrs. E.C. Green, Norwich, Ct." Another small sticker, Library of the 26th Infantry; [and] a rubber stamp, "Post Library Fort McKavett, Texas."

That day, lifting the lid of another box, my eyes caught sight of a sheaf of pages the size of ordinary letter sheets, with this handwriting, "Journal Kept on the Victorio Campaign in 1880 by Robert K. Grierson, A true copy of the original."

I flipped a few pages, saw "wrote to Mama this afternoon." Then saw words that his father was at a dance followed by "I always feel lost at a hop." On another page, "Maj. Woodward gave me a drink of whiskey." "I had a stomach ache today."

Thinks I, this is nonsense, no value. I tossed the sheaf of pages back into the box. Then a thought struck me, a hunch, that the whole thing might have <u>something</u> worth reading, some bit of history, <u>something</u>. So I retrieved the pages and asked Mead Wilson if I might take and copy them. His answer was yes, under consideration that I would return them.

At Scobee's Shack my secretarial wife Katherine typed the Journal, with a carbon copy. It was a long and tiresome chore. I glanced at 2 or 3 pages and was still unimpressed. I thrust them into a letter file. I took the original back to the Big House and saw that Mead Wilson saw me toss it into one of the big boxes of books.

Now this was around 1936. I never laid eyes on those pages again for 19 years. The occasion then was the town's observance of the Fort's 100th birthday, the Centennial. Frank M. Temple, a damn Yank from Massachusetts, came by my office. He was assistant librarian at Texas Tech in Lubbock. He was planning his master's degree work there, and later on asked if I could assist him some on the Grierson angle, as he had chosen Grierson for his thesis. I remembered the Journal, but told him it had no value historically or otherwise, that is was just a youth's fancy ravings. I up and gave him the carbon copy then and there. Soon he wrote me that it was something rare and valuable, entertaining, factual, worth its weight in diamonds! I was not moved to peruse the original copy.

A while after Uncle Sam took over Fort Davis army post in early 1963 as a National Historic Site, a National Park Service historian, Robert M. Utley, came by my office asking to borrow "that journal on the Victorio War written by General Grierson's son." I opened a cabinet, of files, to get the document, and it wasn't there. I did not locate it anywhere, even after some industrious searching.

I told the fort people to write Frank Temple and ask to borrow his copy. He turned them down flat – no siree, Robert's Journal would not leave his hands for any reason to anybody, anywhere! I wrote Frank that the NPS people were honest and that their historians were reliable and lived by historical values and wouldn't he please lend 'em the Journal. He did. The fort people Xeroxed a copy for me also.

My original? About four years ago I came upon a forgotten letter file. In it was the precious original plus some letters and two telegrams from LBJ before he was president, only a Senator, about the appointment of a new postmaster, not me; I was acting in my capacity as County Democratic Chairman for 32 years. Yes sir, or ma'am, I still have it.

As to the phrase, "A true copy of the Original," the only possible explanation, from years of thinking on the subject, and learning that no other Grierson's had ever heard of the Journal, and realizing that Robert may have scribbled his original in the saddle, night call, anywhere, and crudely, it would have fit his character for him have done the "true copy" himself. Which has become my conviction.

Written in the first days of November, 1972, at my home where I am prisoner of a broken hip as of June 12, 1972, but may soon be forgotten, I mean liberated, dismissed, released, or thrown out to descend once again to my courthouse office.

Fort Davis, at 2 p.m., November 3, 1972
Barry Scobee

Chapter One: Robert Grierson and His Family

Robert Kirk Grierson, born December 2, 1860, was the third of seven children born to Benjamin Henry Grierson and Alice Kirk Grierson. Brother Charles was five years older, and a second child, John Kirk, had died at age two. Robert would be followed by Edith Clare (1865), Ben, Jr., called Harry (1867), and Theodore McGregor, "George" (1869). The final child, Mary Louisa (1871) lived only a few months.[1]

From a young age Robert was a brilliant and curious child described by his Aunt Louisa as "One of the most charming little mortals" and "brimming with thought."[2] A precocious child he was quick to question and then challenge the answer. After being told that Robert was convinced that he was a soldier with the rank of major, his grandfather wrote out a commission, signing it with Lincoln's name, and Alice made him a major's uniform. When told to pray for his father each night he asked how "Praying to God could keep the rebels from shooting him."[3] The family home was in Jacksonville, Illinois, which would remain a stable focus throughout Robert's life, especially after the Civil War as the Griersons took station at various frontier posts.

Benjamin H. Grierson and the 10th Cavalry founded Fort Sill, Indian Territory, in January 1869. As construction on the post continued

---

[1] Shirley Leckie, *The Colonel's Lady on the Western Frontier: The Correspondence of Alice Kirk Grierson* (Lincoln: University of Nebraska Press, 1989); William Leckie and Shirley Leckie, *Unlikely Warriors: General Benjamin Grierson and His Family* (Norman: University of Oklahoma Press). The biographies of Grierson and his wife Alice and the history of the family are best told through these books.
[2] Leckie and Leckie, p. 126.
[3] Ibid, p. 129.

Grierson was able to bring his family out. In August 1871 Robert received his first taste of campaigning with his father. Grierson and Ranald MacKenzie, colonel of the 4th Cavalry, had agreed to a mutual operation against the Comanche's on the Staked Plains of the Texas Panhandle. After three weeks of heat and marching through difficult country both contingents returned to base. After this, Robert's first adventure in the field, he and his father returned to Fort Sill to find the new baby, Mary Louisa, ill. She died on September 1, less than three months old.[4]

In April 1875 Grierson took command of Fort Concho. Since there was no school at the post and Robert was obviously an intelligent child, he was left behind in Jacksonville to attend high school. At this point Charles was a cadet at West Point, and these separations were difficult for both the boys and their parents. Robert was living in the Jacksonville home, which was rented to a family who agreed to watch over him. Over part of the winter of 1876-77 he was actually living alone in what his grandfather, John Kirk, called "Bachelor Hall." Kirk, writing to his daughter, stated, "I know not what progress Robt has made during the winter in his studies, as he never lets me see his reports. But he has been out so much at night that I can hardly see how he could make very much progress at school. What Robert needs most, as I think, is to be placed under restraint, to be taught to submit to authority."[5] In contrast, his uncle, John Grierson, wrote Alice that Robert's behavior was no worse than his father's had been at the same age.[6] In his own defense Robert wrote his mother stating, "I'm progressing tolerably well in school. Well,

---

[4] Leckie and Leckie, pp. 191-192.
[5] Shirley Leckie, pp. 100-101.
[6] Leckie and Leckie, p. 239.

I'll tell you how it was in as few words as possible: I cut up too much and I wrote a composition that wasn't liked *too* much. Mr. Block gave me a real good talking to: just what I needed. I can conscientiously say that I did wrong and that I am trying to do right now."[7] Robert returned to Fort Concho for the summer break in July 1877, relieving his mother of much stress.

The concern now was Charles, who had suffered a mental breakdown at West Point, a problem that would also plague Robert later in life. In September 1877 both Charles, with a year's leave from West Point to recover, and Robert were home at Fort Concho, where the family was united for the first time in three years. In May 1878 Robert and Charles accompanied their father on a survey of his district to inspect roads and the other garrisons, Robert's second venture into the field with his father. From mid-May into July the colonel toured the region, passing through Fort Davis for the first time, a post he found to his liking. He wrote to Alice, "I like the post much better than Stockton or even Concho, although the views are a little restricted or confined, yet the scenery is beautiful." He also reported that the commanding officer's quarters were, "a palace compared with the old rat trap at Concho we live in."[8] In September the family was once again devastated by the death of Edith shortly after her thirteenth birthday.

As Robert returned to Jacksonville to complete his schooling, his thoughts turned to the future, and he decided that he wanted to follow brother Charles to West Point. His decision did not sit well with Alice

---

[7] Shirley Leckie, p. 100.
[8] Shirley Leckie, p. 112-113.

who feared that the stress there would affect him as it did Charles. Robert wrote his mother, "I think it is one of the greatest honors a person can have in this country to be a graduate of West Point. I would get such a thorough education and sound drilling that it would be an advantage to me all the days of my life." When Alice expressed opposition to West Point, Robert suggested the Naval Academy as an alternative. Alice wrote, "I never liked the idea of your going to Annapolis, as you know – nor do I think favorably of you going to West Point. We will try and make some satisfactory arrangement for you by the time you graduate from High School"[9]

It is possible that Alice Grierson had reason to be concerned about her son and felt the need to make satisfactory arrangements for him. He had already developed a reputation in Jacksonville with the mothers of his female classmates. Claiming that he was no worse than the other boys in school, he replied to his mother, "I get along pretty well in school and intend to keep on in that way. If I never 'fool with the girls' anymore than I have since I've been away this time I'll do mighty well. It is my aim to do nothing while you are away from me, that I wouldn't do before your face. I here make you this promise and if I *ever* break it may I fall dead on the spot: - I never intend to *say* or *do* anything improper with a girl."[10] However, Robert did continue to care about the girls, and one of his major concerns in his campaign journal was whether or not there would be letters arriving in the mail.

---

[9] Ibid, p. 122.
[10] Shirley Leckie, p. 122-123.

Robert was also interested in more serious concerns and by the summer 1880 he had graduated from high school where the subject of his senior oration was "War and its Influence on Civilization." As he explained to Alice, "It's a pretty big gun to shoot but if I hold it tight I guess the recoil will not hurt me. Such a subject requires lots of thought & reading. I'll do as well as I can. I'll take a big load of study on *the subject before I* pull the trigger."[11] As he would demonstrate during the Victorio campaign, he was not above accepting a challenge.

After graduating he joined the family at Fort Concho, where his father was preparing for a campaign against the Apache under chief Victorio. Robert had been in the field twice before, and there seemed to be little concern about his riding with his father into the desolation of West Texas.[12] On July 10, 1880, with an escort of eight troopers and a telegraph operator, Grierson and his son left for Robert's great adventure.[13]

By 1883, with Alice opposed to either of the service academies, Robert decided on a career in medicine. That fall he entered the University of Michigan Medical School. He did well the first semester, but in January 1884 he suffered a mental breakdown. Confined to the attic in the family home in Jacksonville, he was cared for by his aunt for four months until Alice arrived. She wrote to her husband "We must prepare

---

[11] Ibid, p. 120.

[12] Leckie & Leckie. pp. 251-252. In May 1878 Grierson made an inspection tour of his District of the Pecos. Robert was home from Jacksonville and accompanied his father.

[13] The telegraph would play a major role in the Victorio campaign and Grierson was seldom without an operator with the equipment to "cut into" the line wherever and whenever needed.

ourselves to *look* this Family tendency of Insanity squarely in the face. It has been developed in the first two of our children *now living* and under certain circumstances may or might not show itself in the two younger boys."[14] She thought the causes might be the burden of living away from the family for such long periods and the pressures of obtaining an education without parental support. She determined that neither Harry nor George would be subject to such conditions.

Grierson visited Fort Davis for the second time at the start of the Victorio Campaign. He found the commanding officer's home vacant. Much impressed he wrote Alice, "I am all alone in my glory in the Commanding Officer's Quarters. I have examined the quarters thoroughly. The rooms are well provided with closets, cupboards, wardrobes and are far more comfortable and commodious than our quarters at Concho."[15] Finding the region to his liking, after the Victorio campaign, Grierson moved the headquarters of the 10th Cavalry to Fort Davis in 1881. He immediately began to purchase land and eventually would own a number of sections (640 acres) of prime grazing land that he would stock with cattle and sheep. Robert was now home and recovered enough that his father requested that the quartermaster employ him as forage master for the fort. Those duties required the acquisition of hay and grain for the numerous animals maintained at the post.[16]

In 1884 the 10th Cavalry was transferred to Arizona, where Geronimo was still creating problems. Leaving Fort Davis, the regiment

---

[14] Leckie and Leckie, p. 278.
[15] Benjamin Levy, *Commanding Officer's Quarters, Fort Davis, Texas, Furnishings Study* (Washington: National Park Service, 1968), p. 21.
[16] Leckie and Leckie, p. 20.

was together as a unit for the first time. When the colonel moved his regimental headquarters to Whipple Barracks, Robert was left behind in Fort Davis to manage the family ranching interests.

For a gregarious and intelligent young man this was a boring way of life. "My work is perfect drudgery and is neither beneficial to mind or body," he wrote. He also complained that his circumstances precluded finding a wife, but he felt that returning to Jacksonville was not an option, for he would "rather be shot with a box full of red hot tacks than go there." As a respite he spend Christmas 1885 with the family, now stationed in Santa Fe, and then he and Harry journeyed to San Francisco and Los Angeles for sightseeing. Harry returned to Fort Davis with Robert and remained with his brother until the fall.[17]

On August 16, 1888, Alice Kirk Grierson died after a long illness. Her death only increased Robert's depression. Still living in Fort Davis, he was one of the four county commissioners and, as such, had, with another local citizen, guaranteed the county treasurer's bond. When the treasurer fled with two thousand dollars of the county's money, the other commissioners asked that the funds be made good. Once more the pressure was too great, and Robert suffered another mental break, this one permanent. He spent the rest of his life in mental institutions, dying in1922.[18]

Like many families of the period the Griersons were a diverse group but tight knit and greatly involved in the affairs of the day. In many ways they reflected the attitudes and lifestyle of officers who fought

---

[17] Shirley Leckie, pp. 160-163; Leckie and Leckie, pp. 287-288.
[18] Leckie and Leckie, p. 195 and p. 303; Also see Barry Scobee's Introduction.

during the Civil War and remained in the Regular Army after the conflict. Grierson was encouraged to stay in the army by his wife Alice, and she followed him from one frontier fort to another, with occasional extended visits to the family home in Jacksonville, Illinois.

Benjamin Henry Grierson married Alice Kirk in 1854. She was his childhood friend, and he a gifted musician who taught music. Alice's father, John Kirk, believed in the advancement of women and ensured that she had an education at a time when most young women received virtually none. She bore seven children, but sadly, due to infant mortality and a history of mental illness the family name ended with Benjamin and his children.

The first Grierson in this line, named Robert, arrived in America from Ireland in 1818 with his pregnant wife Mary Shepard and two daughters. The couple settled in Pittsburg, where Robert was a shoemaker and merchant. The couple had seven children, the last of which was Benjamin Henry born on July 8, 1826.[19]

Alice was born to John and Susan Kirk on May 3, 1828, the eldest of thirteen children. Reared in a religious family, Alice faced fierce opposition from her father to her relationship with Grierson, who was completely indifferent towards religion. However, Alice's was faithful to her upbringing and one of her lifelong tasks was to maintain a religious presence in the family.[20]

At one point Ben had hopes of attending West Point, but his mother dissuaded him from that path and encouraged his music career.

---

[19] Leckie and Leckie, pp.3-7.
[20] Ibid, p. 28.

However, when the South seceded from the Union, he did answer the call to arms. Hesitant to join immediately, he studied books on military tactics, and when asked to carry dispatches from his friend Richard Yates, governor of Illinois, to Benjamin Prentiss in Cairo, he did so. Yates appointed Prentiss as brigadier general of state troops, and Grierson found himself in the Union Army when Prentiss appointed him a lieutenant and aide-de-camp at no pay. After living for five months on borrowed money he was finally appointed to a permanent position as major in the 6th Illinois Cavalry. Having been severely injured when he was eight, Grierson was not fond of horses. He asked for a transfer, but General Henry Halleck, commanding the Western Department, refused. Grierson later said, "General Halleck jocularly remarked that I looked active and wiry enough to make a good cavalryman."[21] Indeed he did.

Grierson quickly impressed the men around him with his leadership ability. In April 1862, after thirty-seven regimental officers petitioned Governor Yates, Grierson was promoted to colonel, and in December 1862, General Grant gave him command of a brigade, consisting of three regiments of cavalry: the 6th and 7th Illinois and the 2nd Iowa. With this brigade he would catapult himself into fame, including the cover of *Harper's Weekly*.

As Grant prepared to run the guns at Vicksburg on the Mississippi, Grierson and his men were marching from their base at LaGrange, Tennessee, to disrupt communications and supplies behind the

---

[21] D. Alexander Brown, *Grierson's Raid* (Urbana, University of Illinois Press, 1962), p. 25.

defenses of the beleaguered city.[22] Marching on April 17, 1863, Grierson had under his command 1700 men of his, and six two-pound guns from the 1st Illinois Artillery. The Iowa regiment was under the command of Colonel Edward Hatch, who would remain Grierson friend and command the 9th Cavalry in New Mexico during the first phase of the Victorio Campaign. All three regiments were understrength by half, but this still constituted a major troop movement behind enemy lines.[23]

On April 21 Hatch was detached to destroy the railroad between Columbus and Macon, and then to return to LaGrange, with the expectation of creating even more confusion for the pursuing Rebels. Grierson continued south destroying sections of the Vicksburg and Meridian Railroad and the New Orleans and Jackson Railroad, and arriving at Baton Rouge on May 2. The only significant opposition encountered was Friday, May 1 at Wall's Bridge on the Tickfaw River.[24]

General Grant expressed pleasure at Grierson's success, "It was at Port Gibson I first heard through a Southern paper of the complete success of Colonel Grierson. This raid was of great importance, for Grierson had attracted the attention of the enemy from the main movement against Vicksburg."[25] The Confederate response to the raid, as would be expected, was more restrained. As one Southern Military History reported "as it was, however, Grierson was compelled to make his

---

[22] Tom Lalicki, *Grierson's Raid: A Daring Cavalry Strike through the Heart of the Confederacy* (New York: Farrar, Straus, Giroux, 2004), p. 17.
[23] Brown, p. 19.
[24] Ibid, pp., 191-203
[25] U.S. Grant, Personal Memoirs, edited by Caleb Carr (New York: Modern Library, 1999), p. 536.

trip with such celerity that he did not find time to do much damage."[26] However, the only opinion that mattered was Grant's who reported to General Halleck in Washington that, "Grierson knocked the heart out of the state."[27] The raid cemented Grierson's relationship with Grant and he and his raiders were featured on the cover of *Harper's Weekly* magazine on June 6, 1863.[28] For Grierson's part he enjoyed the adulation, writing home, "My dear Alice, I like Byron have had to wake up in the morning and find myself famous. Since I have been here it has been one continuous ovation. I have received 4 months' pay today and enclosed you will find draft on New York [bank] for $500."[29] As further reward Grierson was promoted to Brigadier General of Volunteers and Chief of Cavalry for Grant's Sixteenth Corps. He would serve in the cavalry for the duration of the war.[30]

By the end of the war and with his appointment as Colonel of the 10th Cavalry, Grierson enjoyed the support and friendship of most of his colleagues, especially Grant and William Tecumseh Sherman. He enjoyed these benefits while Grant was Commanding General of the Army, a post he relinquished to run for president. After Grant was replaced by Sherman, Grierson continued to enjoy the support of the new Army

---

[26] Charles Hooker, Confederate *Military History,* Vol VII (Mississippi) (Atlanta: *Confederate* Publishing *Company,* 1899), p. 133.
[27] Ronald White, *American Ulysses: A Life of Ulysses S. Grant* (New York: Random House, 2016), p. 263.
[28] Lilicki, p. 180.
[29] Ibid. p. 177.
[30] Elizabeth Leonard, *Men of Color to Arms* (New York: W.W. Norton & Company, 2010), pp. 47-8. In late 1864 Grierson led another successful raid into Mississippi, destroying railroad cars and 200 hundred wagons of Confederate supplies.

commander. However, when Philip Sheridan took command of the Army in 1883, Grierson lost his benefactors.

Grierson supported Grant's Indian Policy when many in the Army did not, and he always enjoyed a cordial relationship with Sherman, who wrote of Grierson that he "was one of the most willing, ardent, and dashing cavalry officer I had ever had – always ready, day or night – against equal and *superior foes he handles his men with great skill, doing some of the prettiest* work of the war."[31] However, Grierson did not fare well under Sheridan, who did not appreciate Grierson's conduct as an officer who respected his African American troops and sympathized with the Native Americans he would often have to pursue. With good reason Grierson thought that Sheridan played favorites, especially towards his Civil War companions George Custer and Wesley Merritt, who were equal in rank and ability to Grierson. When Sheridan was dispatched to Texas with a force designed as a warning to Maximilian in Mexico, he replaced Grierson with Custer as commander of the cavalry. In addition Grierson was once again shunted aside during Sheridan's 1868 Washita campaign against the southern plains Indians.[32] It was in one of the ironies of Grierson's career that he sat on the panel of officers during the September 1867 court-martial of Custer.[33] Grierson thought, and rightly so, that Sheridan was blocking his coveted promotion to brigadier general in the Regular Army.

---

[31] Paul Hutton, *Phil Sheridan and His Army* (Norman: University of Oklahoma Press, 1999), p. 227.

[32] Hutton, pp. 228-230. Grierson, not normally a vindictive man, referred to Sheridan as "Sherry-Dan."

[33] T.J. Stiles, *Custer's Trials: A Life on the Frontier* Life *of a New America* (New York: Alfred A. Knopf, 2015), pp. 255-57.

Sheridan died in 1888 and was replaced as commanding general by John Schofield, Grierson's friend. In March 1890, George Crook suddenly died, and this opened a position for major general. When Nelson Miles moved up in rank, there was an opening for brigadier. Finally, on April 5, 1890, three months before his retirement, Grierson was promoted to Brigadier General in the Regular Army and received his star.[34] Benjamin Henry Grierson died on August 31, 1911. A Civil War hero and able post-War commander he brought peace to West Texas. His son Robert, who accompanied his father on the Victorio Campaign, left an indelible record of their adventures in the summer 1880.

---

[34] Leckie and Leckie, p. 303.

Benjamin Henry Grierson
Civil War Major General of Volunteers famous for his raid around the defenses of Vicksburg. Colonel of the Tenth U.S. Cavalry. (Courtesy Fort Davis National Historic Site)

Alice Kirk Grierson
Devoted wife and mother. (Courtesy Fort Davis National Historic Site)

Robert Kirk Grierson
(High School graduation photograph) Of Robert, his father wrote, "who jut
through high school, was out in search of adventure and suddenly found it"
(Courtesy Fort Davis National Historic Site)

Charles Henry Grierson
Eldest son. Second Lieutenant soon after graduation from West Point (1879)
(Courtesy Fort Davis National Historic Site)

May Walcott, Jacksonville, Illinois
*One of the many girls from high school in Jacksonville with whom Robert
corresponded (Courtesy Jacksonville, Illinois Public Library)*

Colonel Edward Hatch, Ninth U.S. Cavalry
Colonel of the 9th Cavalry in New Mexico and commander of the 2nd Iowa Cavalry participating in Grierson's Civil War raid. (Courtesy Fort Davis National Historic Site)

Chapter Two: Victorio's Apache

The word Apache was enough to strike fear throughout the Southwest and northern Mexico. However, as with most Native American cultures, there was no one Apache tribe, in fact, the Apache were among the most diverse in North America. Nevertheless to the Americans relentlessly moving west the Apache represented a barrier that had to be overcome if the course of empire was to continue. As the United States took possession of its new western territories after the Mexican War, the Army, the agency of that possession, encountered a number of Native American peoples but none as fierce and independent as the Apache.

The Apache had no written records and lived in one of the harshest imaginable environments where a nomadic lifestyle was necessary for survival. These circumstances make it difficult to sort out the various groups and relationships. At the time of the first European incursions into the region, the Apache consisted of two major groups, defined geographically. The eastern division included the Jicarillas, Lipans and Kiowa-Apache. The western division was, in turn, divided into four main groups: the Navahos, the Western Apache, the Mescaleros and Chiricahuas. The Chiricahuas ranged from northern Mexico throughout much of Arizona from the Mogollon Rim to the Rio Grande. The Mescaleros, to the east inhabited the area as far as the Pecos River and the mountain ranges of southern New Mexico and West Texas. Within these broader bands there were smaller, discrete units, one of which was called Chihennes. They were a branch of the eastern Chiricahuas, but were most often referred to as Mimbres or Warm

Springs Apache for their preferred home of Ojo Caliente near the present Truth or Consequences, New Mexico.[1]

When the Southwest was under Spanish rule, the Apache developed a lifestyle based upon raiding the more sedentary tribes and frontier Spanish settlements and then using the stolen goods: foodstuffs, slaves, horses and such, as items to trade back to different settlements and tribes. Although the Spanish authorities mounted a number of punitive expeditions into the region they called Apacheria, this raid and trade process was well established by the time the United States took possession of the Southwest 1848 under the Treaty of Guadalupe-Hidalgo, in 1848.[2]

Ranging throughout the Southwest the Apache from all groups came into immediate conflict with the Americans as the nation began to exert authority over its new territories. This inherent tension was greatly increased by the discovery of gold in California and the great rush west that began in 1849. Access to the gold fields was limited by geography, with the established Oregon/California Trail only viable during the warm

---

[1] Kathleen P. Chamberlain, *Victorio: Apache Warrior and Chief* (Norman: University of Oklahoma Press, 2007), pp. 10-14; Dan Thrapp, *Victorio and the Mimbres Apaches* (Norman: University of Oklahoma Press. 1974), pp. 3-4 Thrapp, *Encyclopedia of Frontier Biography* (Lincoln: University of Nebraska Press, 1988), p. 1483. Discussing tribal names, Thrapp writes, "Originally these names may have had valid geographical meaning, but in the jostling about that followed the influx of white settlers such titles became rootless. Thus a name might refer to some small party that happened to camp near the copper mines or along the Mimbres or Gila rivers, or in the vicinity of Warm Springs or Ojo Caliente, rather than to any generic grouping." Chamberlain writes, "If historians have found it difficult to pinpoint the [Apache], it is because their numerous bands remained small, fluid, and extremely mobile. They never traveled as a single unit, but in many extended family groups dubbed *rancherias*."
[2] Chamberlain, pp.20-22.

weather months. The route around Cape Horn was both dangerous and time consuming, while the passage by ship to Panama and the land crossing of the disease-ridden Isthmus in order to find another ship to California was no more desirable. The only all-weather route crossed West Texas, New Mexico, Arizona, and into southern California.

Originally laid out by Army engineers under the command of Lt. Col. Joseph E. Johnston, two primary trails crossed West Texas, meeting in El Paso. The Upper Road originated at Fort Smith, Arkansas, and looped south of the Llano Estacado to Horsehead Crossing on the Pecos River. Following the Pecos the trail turned west through Guadalupe Pass and the Hueco Tanks to El Paso. The Lower Road, also called the Military Road, began at San Antonio, fed by the Gulf of Mexico ports of Galveston and Indianola. This route crossed the Pecos at Live Oak Creek, passed through the Davis Mountains to Van Horn's Wells, and joined the Upper Road at El Paso.[3] This route was protected by a series of forts that included Clark, Lancaster, Stockton, Davis, Quitman, and Bliss at El Paso.

While the mission of these forts was to protect travelers on the road, the Army of the period was ill equipped to do so. With only five mounted regiments for service throughout the country, infantry manned most of these posts, and patrolling the road alone taxed the capabilities of foot soldiers, leaving pursuit into the Apache homeland virtually

---

[3] For a complete explanation of the complicated road surveys across West Texas see: Larry Francell, *Fort Lancaster: Texas Frontier Sentinel* (Austin: Texas State Historical Association, 1999), pp 20-31; and William Goetzmann, *Army Exploration in the American West, 1803-1863,* (New Haven: Yale University Press, 1959), pp. 225-233.

impossible. Mounted troops were required, but in peacetime the Congress was not willing to bear the additional expense.[4]

West Texas was abandoned by the Army during the Civil War, but after the war soldiers returned to West Texas and New Mexico to reclaim many of the posts and return to guarding the road. Circumstances were again ripe for renewed conflict with the Apaches, who still possessed the land and were determined to protect their homes and way of life. At the center of this impending conflict was one of the chiefs of the Warm Springs Apaches, Victorio.

The Chihennes lived in the middle ground between the Chiricahuas to the west and the Mescaleros to the east. Related to and interacting with both, they, however, were a distinct tribe. Their chief Victorio was born sometime between 1820 and 1825 and was estimated to be approximately 55 years of age at his death in 1880. As is sometimes the case with exceptional native leaders, there was a claim that Victorio was actually a Mexican child stolen during a raid on a hacienda in

---

[4] J.D.B. Stillman, *Wanderings in the Southwest in 1855,* ed. Ron Tyler (Spokane, Washington: Arthur H. Clark Company, 1990), p. 143. Stillman, a physician by training, was one of the first travelers to cross the Southwest by stagecoach. For two months, October and November, 1855, he served as the contract post surgeon at Fort Lancaster on the Texas frontier. An astute observer he was quick to understand the problem the Army faced "as for any offensive operations, what can they do without horses, against these Arabs of the American desert? As well might dragoons be used as marines on the deck of a frigate." .p 143. And, "the qualifications for this warfare are endurance, daring, cunning and coolness, and there should be entire freedom to conform to the necessities of the case, to hunt the Indian in his own style; to endure long marches without cooking, without baggage in silence; to hover about the track of the savage where ever it leads; to be a shadow to a shadow." Ibid.

Chihuahua, Mexico. Since there is no oral tradition among the Apaches themselves to back up this claim, it is almost certainly false.[5]

By age twelve or thirteen Victorio would have entered the Apache warrior society being taught by example by the older men in the band. Soon he became an integral part of the hunting and raiding culture. By the end of the U.S. – Mexican War, Victorio had a wife and, soon after, children. The primary Warm Springs chief of this period was Cuchillo Negro, with whom Victorio's name became associated. Cuchillo Negro was, in turn, allied with Mangas Coloradas, considered to be one of the greatest of the Chiricahua leaders and the first important chief to come in contact with the Americans moving into the new territories. The first meeting between the Americans and the Apaches, with Mangas Coloradas as leader, occurred during the U.S. – Mexican War on October 20, 1846, as the "Army of the West" under the command of General Stephen Watts Kearney approached the Gila River. Kearney's command consisted of 300 men of the U.S. First Dragoons, a small artillery detachment, several mountain men enlisted as scouts, including Kit Carson, and a detachment of U.S. Army Topographical Engineers under the command of Major William H. Emory.[6]

---

[5] The most comprehensive biography of Victorio is in Chamberlain, *Victorio: Apache Warrior and Chief*. Other biographical information may be found in Dan Thrapp, *Victorio and the Mimbres Apaches*.

[6] Winston Groom, *Kearney's March: The Epic Creation of the American West, 1846-1847* (New York: Alfred A. Knopf, 2011), p. 139. As part of the overall war strategy, Kearney was ordered to New Mexico. Taking Santa Fe without firing a shot, he left Colonel Sterling Price in command there, sent Colonel Alexander Doniphan with 1000 Missouri Volunteers south towards El Paso, while he proceeded to California.

Major Emory, trained as an engineer at West Point and fourteenth in the class of 1831. Emory would accompany Kearney to California, participate in the events there, and eventually take command of the U.S.-Mexican Boundary Survey, which he brought to a satisfactory conclusion.[7] Emory was a keen observer and his notes from Kearney's march provide one of the first descriptions of the Apache.[8]

John Russell Bartlett, the U.S. Boundary Commissioner who was eventually replaced by Emory, arrived at the copper mines of Santa Rite del Cobre in April 1851. More interested in his personal adventures than the actual survey, his extended his stay and had ample opportunity to observe the Apache. As before, Victorio remained in the background, and Mangas Coloradas was recognized by Bartlett as the primary chief, and while camped at the copper mines, there were two instances in which young Mexican captives asked for rescue by the Americans. Bartlett found the Apache, with few exceptions to be "an ill-formed, emaciated,

---

[7] L. David Norrie, James C. Milligan and Odie B Faulk, *William H. Emory: Soldier Scientist* (Tucson: University of Arizona Press, 1998).

[8] Major William H. Emory, *Notes of a Military Reconnoissance from Fort Leavenworth, in Missouri, to San Diego, in California* (Washington, D.C.: Wendell and Van Benthuysen, 1848), pp 60-61. His descriptions include the following observations. "By this time a large number of Indians had collected about us, all differently dressed, and some in the most fantastical style. The Mexican dress and saddles predominated, showing where they had mostly made up their wardrobe. One had a jacket made of a Henry Clay flag [a political campaign flag with the image of presidential candidate Henry Clay], which aroused unpleasant sensations, for the acquisition, no doubt, cost one of our countrymen his life." "These men have no fixed homes. Their houses are of twigs, made easily, and deserted with indifference." "[Kit] Carson, with a twinkle of his keen hazel eye, observed to me, 'I would not trust one of them.'"

and miserable looking race" who subsisted primarily by raiding and stealing from the Mexicans and Americans on both sides of the border.[9]

From this point forward contact between the American and the various Apache groups increased, generating tension and often conflict. However, Victorio does not appear in the record until April 7, 1853, when, with eleven other chiefs, he signed a provisional peace compact. His name appears as "Victoria" and includes a thumbprint. One of the government witnesses to this compact was Captain John Pope, who three decades later would command the Department of New Mexico and be responsible for the pursuit in that territory during the Victorio Campaign. This compact, a precursor to a treaty never ratified by Congress, included provisions that the Indians would select chiefs to speak for the entire tribe and find permanent settlements. In turn the Federal Government would guarantee tribal lands and supply food, livestock, and trade goods. It was obvious that neither side understood the nature and lifestyle of the other.

The tensions that developed were centered on the requirement by the Federal Government that the Apache settle permanently on reservations, while the Apache desired to continue a semi-nomadic lifestyle and a warrior culture based upon raiding. The added pressure of

---

[9] John Russell Bartlett, *Personal Narrative, 1850-1853* (Chicago: Rio Grande Press, 1965 Reprint), pp. 300-328. Among other descriptions Bartlett noted that, "the Apache nation as a whole is one of the most widely disseminated on the North American Continent, and embraces a great many tribes which are as yet only known to us by name." In another passage he writes, "In saying that certain individuals were fine looking, I speak of mere physical development. I do not think I ever saw a mild or amiable face among them; on the contrary, they all had a treacherous, fiendish look, which well expressed their true character."

more and more Americans moving into or passing through traditional Apache lands only added to this tension.

With the death of Cuchillo Negro, in May 1857 and with Mangas Coloradas aging and then murdered by Federal troops in January 1863, Victorio came to prominence as a leader of the Chihennes. However, there are only two known photographs of Victorio and few written descriptions.[10] A formal census taken by Indian Agent John Shaw in 1876 does provide information about Victorio's family. At that time he was married with five children and four other dependents. One son, named Washington in this census, has a wife but no children.[11]

While West Texas was virtually abandoned by Federal and Confederate armies alike during the Civil War, the balance of the Southwest was under the command of General James Henry Carleton with his California Column and New Mexico Volunteers. Utilizing the skill and knowledge of Kit Carson and the force of arms he rounded up the Navajos and marched them to the reservation at Bosque Redondo near Fort Sumner. He also forced the Mescalero Apache onto the same reservation. As sworn enemies these two tribes did not fare well. In 1865

---

[10] Eve Ball, *In the Days of Victorio: Recollections of a Warm Springs Apache* (Tucson: University of Arizona Press, 1970), p. 41. James Kaywaykla, a member of the group who as a child survived the massacre of Victorio's band at Tres Castillos, provides a typical description of Victorio in ceremonial dress, "A magnificent figure clad in white breech clout and moccasins, heavily beaded appeared. A scarlet blanket was thrown over his left arm; and a scarlet band held his long loose hair in place. Victorio! I had never seen my chief dressed otherwise than his men, and I did not recognize him at first. I had heard Grandmother speak of that blanket – a gift of Manuelito, Chief of the Navajos. Victorio was not as tall as Naiche [a Chiricahua chief, later Kaywaykla's father-in-law], but I think he was the most nearly perfect human being I have ever seen."
[11] Thrapp, *Victorio*, pp. 181-182.

the 500 Mescaleros fled the reservation and by the terms of the Peace Commission of 1867 the Navajos were allowed to return to their traditional homeland at Canyon de Chelly. Meanwhile, the Apache continued their raiding throughout the Southwest.

As the Army returned in force after the Civil War, the region was divided into three separate districts, creating issues for the unity of command, which often worked to the advantage of Victorio and the other bands. West Texas was assigned to the Fifth Military District, which included Louisiana and Texas. New Mexico became a division in the Department of the Missouri, and Arizona a division in the Department of California. For the most part this meant that Victorio and his Warm Springs band became the responsibility of New Mexico and Texas.[12]

While references are few before 1865, by the end of the Civil War Victorio and his two primary associates, the chiefs Loco and Nana, were recognized for their leadership and were much more prominent in the record. As the war ended and settlers once again began to push west, the U.S. Army returned to the area with the mission of protecting the roads and settlements, confining the various Indian tribes on reservations and mediating when the pressure between the two became too great, usually to the detriment of the Native Americans.

As the Army and settlers flowed back into the Southwest after 1865, the horse and cattle herds, both government and private, became fair game for the Apache, and the raids became unremitting. Tensions

---

[12] For an explanation of the often changing and convoluted organization of regional Army Departments, Divisions and Departments see Raphael Thain, *Notes Illustrating the Military Geography of the United States, 1813-1880,* ed. John M. Carroll (Austin: University of Texas Press, 1979).

increased not only between the Native Americans and the Army become, but also between the Army and the settlers, who were seeking grazing land as well as mineral wealth without regard to treaties or traditional Indian lands.[13]

To compound the issue the Bureau of Indian Affairs, charged with management of the various reservations, was part of the Department of Interior, which often worked at cross purposes to the War Department, which was charged with protecting the frontier. Cooperation or conflict depended entirely upon the individuals involved, Indians Agents and Army commanders.[14] These internal policy conflicts meant little to Victorio and his Apache, but had a great impact on where they were to live and how they were treated. The Peace Policy, implemented when U.S. Grant became president in 1868, reinforced civilian control over Indian affairs and affirmed a course of action directed at moving the various tribes to reservations, encouraging agriculture, and providing supplemental provisions, often inadequate and subject to corruption. It was from this date that the inevitable conflict that culminated in the Victorio Campaign began.

In 1868 Victorio and his band were living in the vicinity of Canada Alamosa, near present Monticello, New Mexico, where he and his people hoped to stay. However, on August 17, 1871, Vincent Colyer, a

---

[13] For information on the political situation and the Army response to both civilian complaints and Indian raids see Robert Utley, *Frontier Regulars: The United States Army and the Indian, 1866-1890* (New York: Macmillan Publishing Co.,1973) pp. 162-175 and Monroe Lee Billington, *New Mexico's Buffalo Soldiers, 1866-1900* (Niwot: University of Colorado Press, 1991), pp.3-23.

[14] Robert Wooster, *The Military and United States Indian Policy, 1865-1903* (New Haven: Yale University Press, 1988), pp. 77-86.

member of the Board of Indian Commissioners, visited the area. While Victorio was absent in Mexico, the Commissioner chose the Tularosa Valley ninety miles to the northwest as the future home of the Warm Springs Apache. On May 17, 1872, approximately three hundred Apache from several bands began the trek to Tularosa. By August there were four hundred in residence, but the conditions were so different from Canada Alamosa that by October over one hundred had left. From this point on much of the band's discontent centered on the desire to return to their former home, which Victorio and his people did after experiencing the harsher environment of Tularosa and the lack of concern on the part of the various officials in charge of Indian affairs.[15]

Over the next two years tensions grew and conflict among the Apache, area settlers, and the Army, charged with controlling the former and protecting the latter, intensified. The problem was exacerbated by the fact that often the officials in charge continued to think of the Apache as one tribe, not the several, autonomous bands they had always been. Finally, in 1874 the reservation at Tularosa was closed, and Victorio and his followers were allowed to go back to Canada Alamosa. However, the number of settlers in much of New Mexico had increased and the pressure on the Apache to stay on their reservations and become "civilized," as defined by their government overseers, intensified.

June 1874 the great Chiricahua chief Cochise died. Much like Mangas Coloradas before him, Cochise was often considered to represent all Apache, especially since there was no particular desire on the part of the numerous settlers moving into the territory to separate one band from

---

[15] Chamberlain, pp. 124-134; Thrapp, pp. 144-168.

another. At this point Geronimo became the leader of the Chiricahuas and Victorio took up the mantle of leadership of the Warm Springs. Thus, two distinct groups would emerge. The United States Army would become intimate with both.

In April 1877 in an attempt to end the on-going border depredations, conflict between the settlers and Apache, and the free movement of warrior bands between the San Carlos and Warm Springs reservations, Indian Agent John Clum arrested Geronimo on the Ojo Caliente Reservation. Several days later he also arrested Victorio, and effectively closing the Ojo Caliente Reservation. Other than those who made good their escape, he removed all of the Apache to San Carlos. From this point, Victorio and his band would constantly be on the move and lead the 9th Cavalry and various other units in New Mexico and the 10th Cavalry and support units in Texas on a chase that lasted through the summer of 1880.

Victorio, Leader of the Warm Springs Apache
(Courtesy Fort Davis National Historic Site)

Apache Village
(Courtesy Fort Davis National Historic Site)

Chapter Three: The Tenth Cavalry

In the military reorganization of 1866, Congress authorized the creation of four, initially six, new regiments of African-American soldiers for the Army by an "Act to Increase and Fix the Military Peace Establishment of the United States." This act provided "that to the six regiments of cavalry now in service, there shall be added four regiments, two of which shall be composed of colored men." This added the 7th and 8th Regiments of Cavalry as white units and the 9th and 10th Regiments staffed by African-Americans led by white officers. In addition, four regiments of African-American infantry were added to the Army roster, but these were eventually cut to only two, the 24th and 25th Regiments of Infantry. In 1892 the first biographer of the 10th Cavalry and the retired unit Quartermaster, Lieutenant John Bigelow, Jr., wrote, "the Tenth Cavalry on the 28th day of July, 1866, thus came into being, to join her sister regiments among the elite of the army, and in the years that followed, created for itself a record that cedes primacy to none."[1]

Initially it was planned that the officers of these new regiments would be chosen from those that served with the U.S. Colored Troops during the Civil War, but, ultimately, officers, except the colonels, were chosen like those for any other unit. Company lieutenants were selected from men who served in the war as volunteers, two-thirds of the captains and field-grade officers in the new cavalry regiments came from those serving as volunteers, and one-half of the officers, captain and above, in

---

[1] Major E.L.N. Glass, *The Tenth Cavalry* (Fort Collins, Colorado: Old Army Press), p. 11.

the infantry were volunteers. The commanding General of the Army, U.S. Grant personally selected the regimental colonels.[2]

In August 1866 Grant ordered General Philip Sheridan, commanding the Division of the Gulf and General William T. Sherman, commanding the Division of the Missouri to each organize one of the new regiments of cavalry. Grant already had officers in mind to command these new units. For the 9th Cavalry he recommended Colonel Edward Hatch, and for the 10th he recommended Colonel Benjamin Henry Grierson.[3] Hatch, a native from Maine moved to Iowa in 1855 where he led the 2nd Iowa Cavalry during the Civil War. He took part in the Grierson Raid in 1863 and ended the war as a Major General of Volunteers. Reduced to the post-War rank of colonel he would join the 9th Cavalry, and command in New Mexico during the Victorio Campaign.[4]

With headquarters established at Fort Leavenworth, Kansas, Grierson began the process of organizing the 10th Cavalry. For both Hatch and Grierson the problem was the procurement of officers willing to serve

---

[2] William A. Dobak and Thomas D. Phillips, *The Black Regulars, 1866-1898* (Norman: University of Oklahoma Press, 2001), pp. 25-29. Dobak and Phillips include an excellent chapter on the selection and experience of the officers chosen to command these regiments.

[3] An interesting fact having to do with selecting officers of these regiments has to do with George Custer. Selected as Lieutenant-Colonel for the 9th Cavalry he asked to trade with his rival Wesley Merritt, selected as Lt. Colonel of the 7th Cavalry. The trade was made during which Custer appealed to President Johnson, asking that "I may be appointed Colonel of one of the new infantry regiments, provided I cannot be appointed Col. Of Cavalry, but in which ever branch of service I may be assigned I most respectfully request to be attached to an organization composed of *White* troops as I have served and wish to serve with no other class." J. Stiles, *Custer's Trials: A Life on the Frontier of a New America* (New York, Alfred A. Knoph, 2015), p. 245.

[4] William Leckie, *The Buffalo Soldiers* (Norman: University of Oklahoma Press, 1967), p. 7.

with Black troops, a position often seen as a career killer. However, in both instances these commanders were able to recruit a strong cadre, many of whom would serve with the regiment for years. Lieutenant Samuel Woodward would serve as regimental adjutant, commissary officer, or quartermaster for twenty years. Captains Nicholas Nolan, Louis Carpenter, and Charles Viele were there from the beginning and would lead their companies in the Victorio campaign. Lieutenants Thomas Lebo and William Kennedy would rise in rank to captain and also command companies during the campaign. Lieutenant Robert Smither, originally a company officer, would serve as regimental adjutant.[5]

Organizing his regiment was made infinitely more difficult by the commanding officer of Fort Leavenworth, Brevet Major General William Hoffman, who did not want the Black troops on his post. At one point Grierson had to order that the word "colored" was not to be used in any report and that his command was "simply the Tenth Regiment of Cavalry U.S. Army,"[6] the only title he would ever use in his reports and correspondence. In July 1867 Grierson was relieved to receive the orders that transferred his headquarters to Fort Riley, Kansas. From that time until the regiment shipped to Cuba during the Spanish-American War, the 10th Cavalry would remain on the frontier, usually in harm's way.

During the Civil War the Army had little presence on the frontier, but in 1867, in an effort to reassert dominance, General Winfield Scott Hancock, Commanding Officer, Department of the Missouri, launched a

---

[5] Glass, pp. 13-14.
[6] Leckie and Leckie, p. 148.

campaign into the southern and central plains. The 10th Cavalry was soon involved. Assigned to guard the construction parties and the line of the Kansas Pacific Railroad, the regiment saw its first action on August 2, 1867, along the Saline River near Fort Hays, Kansas. In a six hour fight Company F engaged a superior force with one officer wounded and a sergeant killed. With only two officers and thirty-four men, the company was forced to retire after inflicting unknown casualties, but the 10th had been bloodied in action, the first engagement of the many to come.

The 10th Cavalry's willingness to fight had been witnessed by no better observer than Elizabeth Custer at Fort Wallace, Kansas, June, 1867. When an estimated three hundred Cheyenne's under Chief Roman Nose attacked elements of the 7th Cavalry, several African-American soldiers assigned to guard and picket duty decided to join the fray. Elizabeth Custer wrote that, "while the fighting was going on, the two officers in command found themselves near each other on the skirmish-line, and observed a wagon with four mules tearing out to the line of battle. It was filled with Negroes, standing up, all firing in the direction of the Indians. The driver lashed the mules with his black snake, and roared at them as they ran. When the skirmish-line was reached, the colored men leaped out and began firing again. No one had ordered them to leave their picket station, but they were determined that no soldiering should be carried on in which their valor was not proved."[7] She identifies neither the officers who participated in this action nor the regimental unit involved.

---

[7] John M. Carroll (ed.), *The Black Military Experience in the West* (New York: Liveright Press, 1971), p. 189.

These early encounters by the 10th were part of a larger campaign conceived by regional department commander Major General Phillip H. Sheridan and the Commander-in-Chief of the Army, General William T. Sherman, to pacify the Indians of the southern plains, specifically the Cheyennes and Arapahos. On September 15, 1868, Company I engaged in a fire fight with an estimated one hundred Cheyenne at Big Sand Creek, and later in the month Companies I and H rode to the rescue of Major George A. Forsyth, who was besieged by several hundred Cheyenne and Sioux on Beecher's Island on a dry tributary of the Republican River. Forsyth, in command of fifty volunteers, mostly experienced frontiersmen, was initially attacked on September 17th and retreated to Beecher's Island to establish a strong defensive perimeter. The siege lasted seven days before relief would arrive in the form of Captain Louis Carpenter and his troopers of the 10th Cavalry.[8]

Captain Carpenter with his Company H and Captain George W. Graham's I Company once more took the field on October 14, 1868 to escort Major Eugene Carr, 5th Cavalry, to his command, which was expected to be at Beaver Creek in the northwestern part of Kansas. Approaching that location the troops were attacked by several hundred Cheyenne. Under attack, Carpenter moved his command to a suitable location, circled his wagons, and, with his dismounted troops using the wagons for cover was able to hold off the attackers. This defensive position proved to be so strong that the Indians, after several were killed and wounded, broke off the attack and retreated. For their gallantry these

---

[8] The campaign of 1868-69 on the southern plains is covered in Utley, *Frontier Regulars*, pp. 142-159. The Beecher Island fight is described in Utley, pp.147-148 and in Glass, p. 16 and William Leckie, pp. 34-35.

men of the 10th Cavalry were specifically thanked by General Sheridan in a field order, and Captain Carpenter was brevetted to Colonel and Captain Graham to major. In 1898 Captain Carpenter was awarded the Medal of Honor for his actions at Beecher's Island and Beaver Creek.[9]

One explanation for the delay in recognizing Carpenter with the Medal of Honor is presented in an 1897 document once belonging to Captain Robert G. Smither of the 10th Cavalry. The author is unknown, but the writer states that "credit for the relief of Colonel Forsythe, was by a strange miscarriage of justice not given at the time as it should have been to Colonel [his rank in 1897] Carpenter and the brave men who followed his splendid leadership. But as the truth finally burns its way through to daylight, recognition and credit came at last, and the true hero of this relief now enjoys an honor which can never be taken from him."[10] This statement may well sum up the issues the Buffalo Soldier regiments faced throughout their history.

It was during these plains campaigns of 1867-69 that the African-American troops received the sobriquet "Buffalo Soldiers." The true meaning and origin of the nickname is lost to history, or at least not well enough known to provide a definitive answer. It is generally agreed that the name came from the Indians sometime during the plains campaigns around 1870. While there are no contemporary accounts from the soldiers themselves, the term first appears in print, October1873, in an article in

---

[9] Francis B. Heitman, *Historical Register and Dictionary of the United States Army*)Urbana: University of Illinois, Press, 1965), p. 284 and Glass, p. 16.
[10] *Roster of Non-Commissioned Officers of the Tenth Cavalry* (St. Paul, Minnesota: Kennedy Printing Company, 1896), (Edited by Douglas McChristian and reprinted by J.M. Carroll & Company, Mattituck, NY, 1983), p. 29.

the *Army and Navy Journal* by an unnamed author. While the author is unknown, the article was sent from Fort Sill, Oklahoma, and stated, "The colored troops (called by the Comanche's 'Buffalo Soldiers,' because like the buffalo, they are wooly) are in excellent drill and condition." He continued, "these 'Buffalo Soldiers' are active, intelligent, and resolute men; perfectly willing to fight the Indians, whenever they are called upon to do so, and appear to me to be rather superior to the average white men recruited in time of peace." It was this latter statement that probably kept the author anonymous, especially considering the number of replies in the *Journal* expressing a contrary opinion.[11]

The first actual use of the term "Buffalo Soldier" was in letters by Francis Roe, wife of Lieutenant Fayette Washington Roe of the 3rd Infantry stationed at Camp Supply, Indian Territory. However, her letters were not published until 1909 in *The Nation*, a popular magazine. In one letter she wrote, "The officers say that the negroes make good soldiers and fight like fiends. The Indians call them 'Buffalo Soldier' because their wooly heads are so much like the matted cushion that is between the horns of the buffalo."[12] Regardless of the term's origin, the Black troops took the name as their own, especially the Tenth Cavalry, which placed the image of a buffalo prominently on its regimental patch and coat of arms.

Sheridan's relentless campaign of pursuit, especially his keeping his troops in the field through the fall and into winter of 1868, drove a

---

[11] Frank N. Schubert, *Voices of the Buffalo Soldiers* (Albuquerque: University of New Mexico Press, 2003), p. 47.
[12] Schubert, pp. 47-48. Excerpts from several of Roe's letters are included herein.

number of the Indians to Fort Cobb under the protection of the army. Fort Cobb was not good shelter for the thousands of soldiers and Indians that were now camped there, and Sheridan determined to locate a more acceptable post and reservation. To do so he chose Colonel Grierson and the 10th Cavalry to construct a new fort on the eastern slope of the Wichita Mountains. This fort was originally established as Fort Wichita on January 7, 1869, but the name was changed to Fort Sill on July 2 in honor of General Joshua Sill, killed at the battle of Stone River, Tennessee, in 1862. Fort Sill became the Indian Agency for the Comanche, Kiowa, Wichita, and several other tribes, as well as Army headquarters for the southern plains.[13]

It was at Fort Sill, in the midst of building a post and attempting to control several unruly tribes that Colonel Grierson created the regimental band. He did this by seeking out men who could read and write and then teaching them music. He often instructed them himself and sought to enlist a qualified leader he could assign permanently to the task.[14]

In spring 1871, the Commanding General of the Army, William Tecumseh Sherman, was on a tour of western forts, and stopped at Fort Richardson in north Texas. On May 19 a wounded teamster arrived at the post with the news of an attack on a wagon train hauling supplies to Fort Griffin. Setting Ranald Mackenzie, Colonel of the 4th Cavalry, in pursuit, Sherman continued on to Fort Sill where he met his old friend Benjamin Grierson. While Sherman was at Fort Sill, on May 27, the Kiowas arrived

---

[13] Robert Frazer, *Forts of the West* (Norman: University of Oklahoma Press, 1972), p. 124.
[14] Glass, p. 18.

for the distribution of rations. Included were the chiefs Satanta, Satank, and Big Tree.

Troopers from the 10th Cavalry were able to peacefully arrest all three chiefs. They were held in the guardhouse until turned over to Colonel Mackenzie, who was to escort them to Texas and hand them over to civil authorities there. Shortly after leaving Fort Sill Satank used a concealed knife to wound a trooper and seize his carbine. He was killed by the escort. Satanta and Big Tree were delivered to Fort Richardson, where they were tried and sentenced to hang. The two were reprieved by Governor Edmund Davis and given life sentences.[15]

In spring 1873 individual companies of the regiment began to transfer to Texas, as well as maintaining their stations in Indian Territory. By spring 1874 the Comanche, Kiowa, and Cheyenne initiated a series of attacks throughout the southern plains portion of Indian Territory and northern Texas into the Panhandle, including an attack on the trading post at Adobe Walls. These depredations reached such a level that General Sherman declared what was basically a state of war against the southern plains tribes. In the ensuing campaign the units of the 10th Cavalry would participate in their first large scale action, which would give them the experience they would need in the chase of the Apache Victorio.[16]

The strategy for the Red River War would be that of the commander of the forces in the west, Lieutenant General Philip Sheridan.

---

[15] Leckie, *Buffalo Soldiers,* pp. 57-63. Leckie explains this episode as important to the history of the Tenth Cavalry whereby the troopers carried out their orders in an orderly and expeditious manner, thus impressing General Sherman.

[16] The story of the Red River War is best told in Utley, *Frontier Regulars,* pp. 219-233 and William Leckie, pp. 113-140.

Pursuing the concept of total war as he had done in the Shenandoah Valley during the Civil War, Sheridan anticipated a winter campaign and columns converging in the area south of the Canadian River and north of the Pease River on the Comanche stronghold of Palo Duro Canyon.[17]

In Sherman's plan Colonel Nelson Miles, with units of his 5th Infantry and troopers from the 6th Cavalry was to march southward from Kansas, while Major William Price, with troopers from the 8th Cavalry was to march east from New Mexico. Colonel Ranald Mackenzie, stationed at Fort Concho with his 4th Cavalry, in conjunction with Lieutenant Colonel George Buell and part of the 11th Infantry was to converge from the east. To the northeast Lieutenant Colonel John Davidson was to march from Fort Sill with troopers from the 10th Cavalry. During this time Colonel Grierson was on recruiting duty at St. Louis, so Davidson took temporary command of the regiment.

Before Davidson could march, there was a minor uprising at the Anadarko Agency, including some of the Indians who were the subject of Sherman's campaign. A fire fight ensued, and, once again, Captain Carpenter distinguished himself by dispersing the hostiles.[18]

This massive concentration of troops was expected to encounter approximately 1000 warriors from the Comanche, Kiowa, and Cheyenne tribes. On August 30, 1874, Miles was the first to encounter the Indians along the Caprock Escarpment below the Staked Plains. In a running fight of five hours, he exhausted his ammunition and supplies and was forced to withdraw towards his supply base. On September 9 a force of 250

---

[17] Joseph Wheelan, *Terrible Swift Sword: The Life of General Philip H. Sheridan* (Cambridge, MA: Da Capo Press, 2012), pp. 267-269.
[18] Glass, p. 20.

Indians, many of them recently driven away from the Anadarko Agency, attacked Miles's supply train near the Washita River in a fight that lasted three days. In the meantime, Major Price was also attacked, but the Indians soon scattered.

On September 26 it was Mackenzie's turn. He was attacked along the eastern caprock at Tule Canyon, but his troopers drove off the hostiles. Although firing continued through the night as the Indians tried to get at the cavalry mounts, in the morning the troopers were able to drive them off. In the interim Mackenzie's scouts had discovered the main Indian camp along the Prairie Dog Town Fork of the Red River in the Palo Duro Canyon. Scrambling down the steep escarpment, a troop at a time the soldiers attacked in column as they hit the bottom of the canyon. With little resistance the Indians fled, and Mackenzie was able to capture the entire camp and horse herd. Both losses proved devastating to the Indians. Mackenzie had his troopers burn the camp and supplies and after selecting the best ponies for his men he had the rest killed, over 1,000.[19]

By this point the region swarmed with troops; several more camps were burned, and the Indians were forced to move continuously. As bitter winter weather set in the various columns returned to their camps by January 1875, and many of the Indians, without food or shelter began to return to the various agencies. For the most part the role of the 10th Cavalry in this campaign was patrolling the sectors assigned. They were not engaged until the final act, when on April 6, 1875, at the Cheyenne Agency, Companies D and M were engaged in a fire fight that included

---

[19] Utley, *Frontier Regulars*, pp. 225-226; Wheelan, p. 271.

Company M of the 6th Cavalry. A group of approximately 150 Cheyenne attempted an escape and fortified themselves on a small sand hill. After holding off the troopers for a day, they eventually fled north and would not be apprehended until they reached Kansas, some four hundred miles from the agency.[20]

On April 30, 1875, Colonel Grierson returned from recruiting duty and established his headquarters at Fort Concho. By this time all of the 10th Cavalry was now stationed in Texas, but scattered from Fort Griffin in the north to Fort Stockton and Davis to the west. Regimental headquarters would remain at Fort Concho for the next seven years until moved to Fort Davis in 1882.[21] However, much of the action over these years would take place in far West Texas and southern New Mexico.

From the move to Texas until the end of the Victorio campaign the 10th Cavalry would stand as protectors of the frontier by consistently patrolling thousands of miles, "in a long succession of hikes and pursuits, with now and then a consoling skirmish with Indians or desperadoes. Their trails led them far into Mexico; into and over the grim fastness of the Guadalupe Mountains; across the deserts of the Staked Plains, the Bad Lands of the Rio Grande and the Big Bend."[22] During this period there were numerous small encounters and several incursions into Mexico.[23]

It was not so much the Indians that created troubles for the 10th Cavalry at Fort Concho but the civilians who did not take well to the presence of the Black troops. The closest community was Saint Angela,

---

[20] Leckie, pp. 135-140.
[21] Glass, p 20.
[22] Ibid.
[23] William Leckie, pp. 141-162. This period from the move to Texas to the Victorio campaign is well documented here.

which Colonel Grierson described as a "resort for desperate characters …

mainly made up of gambling and drinking saloons and other disreputable

places."[24] The conflicts were minor until the fall of 1877 when a group of

Texas Rangers rode into town and stopped at Nasworthy's Saloon. There

they encountered several soldiers from the fort and took umbrage at these

men also dancing and drinking. The Rangers managed to pistol whip

several of the troopers. Grierson asked for an explanation and apology

from the Ranger Captain John S. Sparks, but neither was forthcoming.

The troopers decided to take matters in hand and returned to Nasworthy's

and shot up the place, killing a bystander.

Several months later another incident occurred at Morris' Saloon,

where some cowboys and hunters surrounded a sergeant and cut off his

chevrons and his trouser stripes. Humiliated, the sergeant returned to the

post, gathered several of his men and returned to the saloon. In the

ensuing gunfight, a hunter was killed, with two others wounded, and one

trooper was killed. The result of these incidents was severe punishment

for the men of the 10th and none for the civilians involved.[25]

During this period events in New Mexico and along the Rio

Grande in far West Texas were moving towards what would become the

Victorio Campaign. This would embroil the Buffalo Soldiers in their

greatest endeavor during the Indian Wars, but it was only after this

campaign was over that the regiment came together for the first time as a

unit. On April 1, 1885 the eleven troops of the regiment, with the band

---

[24] Ibid., p. 163.
[25] William Leckie, pp. 163-154. For a blatantly racist account of these
incidents see J. Evetts Haley, *Fort Concho and the Texas Frontier* (Midland,
TX: West Texas Lagacy Press, 2006), pp. 262-284.

playing, marched out of Fort Davis for station in Arizona. In route they picked up Troop I at old Fort Hancock along the Rio Grande and were together for the first time for the march to Fort Bowie, where they were once again dispersed for frontier duty.

Five years earlier in his annual *Report* to the Secretary of War in 1880, General Edward O.C. Ord, Commander, Department of Texas was asked that the 10th be stationed somewhere other than the frontier. Concerned about the well being of the troops, Ord wrote, "In this connection I beg to invite attention to the long and severe service of the Tenth Cavalry, in the field and at remote stations, in this department. Is it not time that it should have relief by a change to some more favored district of the country?"[26] The regiment would remain on the frontier until 1898.

The regiment would not again be together as a unit until the Spanish- American War.[27] In Arizona the regiment chased Geronimo, and then in 1892 the regiment was transferred to Montana, where it would end its Indian Wars service.[28] The ultimate fame for the 10th Cavalry came on July 1, 1898, during the Spanish-American War, with their charge up San Juan Hill with Teddy Roosevelt's Roughriders.

---

[26] General Edward O.C. Ord, "Annual Report," in the *Annual Report of the Secretary of War for the Year 1880, Volume I* (Washington: Government Printing Office, 1880), p. 111.

[27] Douglas McChristian. *Garrison Tangles in the Friendless Tenth: The Journal of First Lieutenant John Bigelow, Jr., Fort Davis, Texas* (Mattituck, NY: J.M. Carroll & Company, 1885), p. 82.

[28] Glass, pp. 24-93. This section of Glass covers the history of the regiment through World War I, including the Spanish-American War, the Philippine Insurrection, and the Mexican Punitive Expedition.

Captain Nicholas Nolan, Company A
Nolan, born in Ireland, enlisted in the Army in 1852 and was promoted from the ranks to officer in the Civil War. He joined the 10th Cavalry at its formation.
(Courtesy Fort Davis National Historic Site)

Lieutenant Henry O. Flipper, Company A
The first African American to graduate from West Point, Flipper served under Captain Nolan and made the 98 mile ride in 22 hours to warn Grierson that Victorio had crossed into Texas. (Courtesy Fort Davis National Historic Site)

Captain Charles Delavan Viele, Company C
Joining the Union Army in 1861, Viele rose to the rank of captain. He joined the 10th Cavalry in 1870. (Courtesy Fort Davis National Historic Site)

Captain Alexander S.B. Keyes, Company D
From an Army family, Keyes joined the Union Army in 1863. Rising from the ranks, he was promoted to lieutenant and assigned to the 10th Cavalry as a Captain in 1873. (Courtesy Fort Davis National Historic Site)

Captain Louis H. Carpenter, Company H
Carpenter joined the Union Army in 1861, rose from the ranks to colonel by the end of the War. He joined the , enlisted in the Army in 1852 and was promoted from the ranks to officer in the Civil War. He joined the 10th Cavalry at its formation. (Courtesy Fort Davis National Historic Site)

Lieutenant William H. Beck
Beck, who served with Grierson since 1862, was the colonel's aide-de-camp throughout the campaign. (Courtesy Fort Davis National Historic Site)

Lieutenant Geno Smither, Regimental Adjutant
*Smither, who served with Grierson during the Civil War in Mississippi, rose
from the ranks and during the Victorio Campaign was the Regimental Adjutant.
(Courtesy Fort Davis National Historic Site)*

Captain John Curtis Gilmore, Twenty-fourth Infantry (Army Tactical Board, Gilmore standing to the right)
Awarded the Medal of Honor for valor at the Battle of Salem Heights May 3, 1863, Gilmore was in command at Eagle Springs and sent Lt. Flipper on his famous ride. While not an officer of the 10th Cavalry, his troops also supplied the escort for the supply train that was attacked at Rattlesnake Springs and repulsed. (Courtesy Fort Davis National Historic Site)

Dismounted Drill on the Parade Ground, Fort Davis
(Courtesy Fort Davis National Historic Site)

Mounted Troops on Parade, Fort Davis
(Courtesy Fort Davis National Historic Site)

A Campfire Sketch, **Frederic Remington,** *Century* **Magazine**
(Author's Collection)

A Pool in the Desert, **Frederic Remington,** *Century* **Magazine**
(Author's Collection)

Marching on the Mountains, **Frederic Remington,** ***Century*** **Magazine**
(Author's Collection)

Chapter Four: The Victorio Campaign in New Mexico: The Chase Begins

In 1875, while the 10th Cavalry was transferring to Texas, the 9th Cavalry, commanded by Colonel Edward Hatch was moving from Texas to New Mexico replacing, the 8th Cavalry, which in turn took station in Arizona.[1] Hatch, as commander of the 2nd Iowa Cavalry, had participated in Grierson's Raid around Vicksburg and chose to remain in the Regular Army after the War. In 1866 he was responsible for organizing the 9th Cavalry and commanded the regiment for twenty-three years, dying on April 11, 1889, at Fort Robinson, Nebraska.[2] Hatch, born in Maine and educated at the Vermont Military School, had gone to sea as a young man but did not enjoy the experience and went west in 1854 settling in Muscatine, Iowa. He happened to be in Washington, D.C. the day the Civil War started and spontaneously joined a group of volunteers guarding the White House and government buildings. Upon his return to Iowa he was commissioned a Lieutenant and helped organize the 2nd Iowa Cavalry, eventually taking command.[3]

The regiment's arrival in New Mexico coincided with what would be five years of almost constant conflict with Victorio and his band of Warm Springs Apache. In its charge to protect New Mexico the 9th

---

[1] Frank N. Schubert, *Black Valor: Buffalo Soldiers and the Medal of Honor, 1870-1898* (Wilmington: Scholarly Resources, Inc., 1997), p. 41.

[2] Heitman, p. 510 and Robert Girardi. *The Civil War Generals* (Minneapolis, Minnesota: Zenith Press, 2013), p. 82. Grierson described his friend Hatch as follows: "I looked upon him as a brave, discreet, and capable officer: one whose whole heart was thoroughly aroused in the cause of his country." In addition, Hatch, New Mexico, famous for its chili's, was named for the colonel of the 9th Cavalry. Julyan, *Place Names, p.162.*

[3] Brown, *Grierson's Raid,* pp. 61-63.

Cavalry was severely handicapped by numbers and distance. While the regiment had an authorized strength of 840, at any given time Hatch usually had not much more than half that number available. The companies only mustered an average of 56 men. With these limited resources the regiment was expected to cover a vast territory that possessed limited means of communication.[4]

In May 1877, after the closure of the Ojo Caliente Reservation, the Warm Springs Apache did not take well to the San Carlos Reservation. Over time many, including Victorio, slipped away into the mountains. Those who did stay found themselves in conflict with the other bands over limited resources. Initially eight companies of the 9th Cavalry were sent in search of Victorio. Not equipped for the winter, Victorio turned up at Fort Wingate, Arizona, in October seeking shelter. He asked to not return to San Carlos, but to go once again to Ojo Caliente, a request post commander Lieutenant-Colonel Peter Swaine, 15th Infantry, honored.[5]

This respite did not last long; the Army again removed the Apache at Ojo Caliente, and sent them back to San Carlos. Again, Victorio escaped with 80 followers. In June 1878 this band arrived at the Mescalero Reservation where Indian Agent Frederick Godfroy promised shelter. Soon after this the remainder of the Warm Springs Apache were transferred from San Carlos to the Mescalero Reservation, located in the White and Sacramento Mountains in south central New Mexico near Tularosa.[6]

---

[4] Billington, p. 46.
[5] Billington, pp. 53-54; Heitman, p. 938. Peter Tyler Swaine, often misspelled "Swain," was recognized for gallantry at Shiloh and Murfreesboro Hand retired in 1895 as colonel of the 22nd Infantry.
[6] Billington, p. 54; Julyan, p. 226.

However, by the end of the summer of 1878 Victorio was again on the move, taking his people back to Ojo Caliente in the hope of finally settling there. Tired of these maneuvers, the Army decided to move the entire tribe back to San Carlos. On October 8, 1878, two companies of the 9th Cavalry, with a group of Indian Scouts under the command of Captain Frank Tracy Bennett, arrived at Ojo Caliente, New Mexico, to force the removal.[7] Victorio and approximately 100 of his followers decamped for Mexico, and he was not heard from again until he crossed the border early in 1879. Thus began a two year war that raged across New Mexico and West Texas and came to be known as the Victorio Campaign.[8]

For most of 1879 and 1880 the 9th Cavalry, with other units, would search for Victorio and other renegades who were in conflict with the government's reservation policy. While Colonel Hatch was in overall command of the District of New Mexico, field operations primarily fell to Major Albert Marrow, a highly capable officer dedicated to the task at hand.[9] The many patrols throughout the region led mostly to naught, but the Apache were occasionally brought to bay as they continued their hit-and-run tactics against small ranches and travelers. The first of these

---

[7] Heitman, p. 211. Bennett began his military career as an enlisted man in the Civil War. He was promoted to officer for gallantry at Hoover's Gap, Tennessee and ended the war with the rank of captain. He was one of a number of non-West Pointers who chose to serve with the Buffalo Soldiers. In 1889 he retired with the rank of major, and he died in 1894.

[8] Billington, pp. 54-.55.

[9] Heitman, p.729. Morrow, a non-West Pointer, rose through the ranks from sergeant to colonel in the Pennsylvania Volunteer Infantry during the Civil War. Posted briefly to the 7th Cavalry after the War, he transferred to the 9th Cavalry in 1867 and retired as colonel of the 3rd Cavalry in 1892.

encounters occurred in June when Captain Charles Beyer[10] and his Company C, fifteen men from Company I, and several scouts encountered Victorio and his band in the Mimbres Mountains.[11]

The Apache held the high ground. At first Victorio, waving a white flag, tried to persuade Beyer to come to his camp and talk. When this failed, Beyer sent his scouts to capture the herd of horses and mules. Moving skirmishers up slope, Beyer also sent Sergeant Delmar Penn and men from Company I to threaten the Apache right flank. A sharp firefight ensued, and Penn, with enfilading fire, forced Victorio to abandon his works and retreat. Private Frank Dorsey of Company C was killed, and two others were wounded. The number of Indians killed or wounded was unknown.[12]

On June 30, with his animals captured and supplies burned by Beyer, Victorio surrendered once again at the Mescalero Reservation. In less than a month he jumped the reservation, and immediately the 9th Cavalry took up the pursuit. On September 4, 1879, the Apache attacked first when Victorio and about 60 warriors struck the horse herd of

---

[10] Heitman, p. 216. Beyer, an enlisted man and musician before the Civil War rose to the rank of lieutenant serving with the United States Colored Infantry at the end of the War. He then served with the Buffalo Soldiers until dismissed from service in 1884, dying in 1898.

[11] Julyan, p. 41, The Mimbres Mountains are part of the Black Range in the Aldo Leopold Wilderness of the Gila National Forest on the western New Mexico border with Arizona. If one wants to understand the beauty and ruggedness of the Black Range, drive New Mexico 152 west from Caballo on I-25 through Hillsboro and Kingston to Silver City.

[12] Schubert, pp. 50-53, p. 58. On January 6, 1882, Sergeant Thomas Boyne, Company C, 9th Cavalry, was awarded the Medal of Honor for his action in saving Lieutenant Henry H. Wright of the same troop. Wright had his horse shot out from under him and was surrounded by hostiles when rescued by Boyne.

Company E at Camp Ojo Caliente. Five troopers and three civilians guarding the herd were killed. The raiders made off with 18 mules and 50 horses, essentially unhorsing Captain Ambrose Hooker's company.[13]

In his annual report to Congress, General John Pope, commanding the Department of the Missouri, commented, "of course there must have been more or less carelessness on the part of Captain Hooker, Ninth Cavalry, who was in command of the company at the time, but it may be said that the horses were being herded in sight of the post, and that the outbreak of the Indians was wholly unexpected."[14] From this point the pursuit would be relentless. Hatch put all of his men in the field, where they would, in essence, stay for the next twelve months. Including detachments from other regiments and scouts, over 1000 men blanketed New Mexico seeking the elusive Victorio, whose band of warriors never numbered more than one hundred.[15]

In the six days after the attack on Company E's horse herd, the Apache killed nine civilians. Then in September the trail was discovered by the troops of Captain Byron Dawson's Company B and Hooker's remounted Company E.[16] Under the command of Lt. Col. Nathan A. M.

---

[13] Billington, p. 89; Heitman, p. 540. Hooker served with the California Volunteer Cavalry during the Civil War, joining the 9th Cavalry with its formation in 1867.

[14] General John Pope, "Annual Report to the Secretary of War, Headquarters Department of the Missouri," in the *Annual Report of the Secretary of War for the Year 1880, Vol. I* (Washington, Government Printing Office, 1880), p. 86. (Google Books)

[15] Billington, p. 90.

[16] Heitman, p. 361. Dawson, another officer who rose from the ranks of the volunteers during the Civil War, was from Indiana, joining the 9th Cavalry upon its organization. He won brevets for gallant service in actions against Indians along the Pecos River and Brazos River in 1869.

Dudley this column pursued Victorio for two days before reaching the headwaters of Las Animas Creek, a small water course on the east side of the Black Range.[17] There the troops found the Apache once again forted up on higher ground. Dudley found himself in an untenable position but was reinforced by Captain Charles Beyer, Company C, and Lieutenant William H. Hugo, Company G.[18] Beyer and Hugo were scouting in the area and rode to the sound of Dudley's guns, but all four companies now engaged were unable to dislodge Victorio from his works. Dudley withdrew his troops at nightfall with five dead troopers, three dead scouts, and thirty-two dead horses.[19] Lt. Matthias W. Day and Sergeant John Denny would in this encounter later receive the Medal of Honor for rescuing a wounded private named Freeland.[20]

Colonel Hatch replaced his field commander Dudley with Major Albert Morrow. Of Morrow and the campaign that continued, General John Pope, commander of the Department of the Missouri, wrote, "The pursuit was kept up by Major Morrow with unabated persistence and

---

[17] Heitman, p. 386. Dudley served in the regular Army before the Civil War and commanded Massachusetts troops during the war, rising to the rank of Brigadier General of Volunteers. He joined the 9th Cavalry in 1876 and retired as colonel of the 6th Cavalry in 1889.

[18] Heitman, p. 553. Hugo served with New York volunteers during the Civil War, choosing to remain in the Army after the war. After transferring from the 25th Infantr, he served with the 9th Cavalry from 1871 until dismissed from the service in 1881.

[19] William Leckie, pp. 210-211; Billington, p. 91.

[20] Heitman, p. 362; Schubert, *Black Valor,* p.54-56 and p. 117. Lt. Day was not actually awarded the Medal of Honor until May 1990, and Sgt. Denny did not actually receive his until 1991. Day's citation in part read, "In singly advancing into the enemy's line and carrying a wounded soldier of his company on his back down a rocky trail under hot fire after he had been ordered to retreat." Private Freeland recovered from his wounds and was back in the field by October.

vigor, but, though many skirmishes occurred, no decisive fight with the Indians could be forced. The service, in such country and under such circumstances, was extremely hard both upon men and animals, and Major Morrow and his command are entitled to the highest consideration for the determined and persistent manner in which they met and surmounted the difficulties of the pursuit, difficulties due to the utter desolation of the country, and not the prowess of the Indians."[21] The latter statement may well be an exaggeration.

Morrow did, in fact, keep up field operations that lasted without respite for many weeks. On September 8, 1879, Victorio attacked the U.S. Mail and its escort of a sergeant and eight troopers, but all escaped unharmed. The next day, Morrow and his detachment encountered Victorio near Cuchillo Negro Creek, where a two-day fight developed.[22] Finally forced to retreat, Victorio was pursued several miles before the troops returned to the creek for water. In this fight two soldiers were killed, as well as three Apache. Two days later, October 1, Morrow discovered the Indian camp. After placing his troops for an attack at daylight, Morrow discovered that Victorio had already made good his escape.[23]

On October 4 Morrow resupplied at Ojo Caliente and immediately returned to the pursuit with over one hundred men, mostly troopers from the 9th Cavalry, but also a detachment from the 6th Cavalry and twenty-

---

[21] Pope,in the *Annual Report of the Secretary of War,1880,* p. 86.
[22] Julyan, p. 103. Cuchillo Negro Creek flows from the Black Range southeast into the Rio Grande north of Truth or Consequences (Hot Springs, New Mexico). Named for a former chief of the Warm Springs Apache the name means "Black Knife."
[23] William Leckie, p. 211-212.

five Indian scouts. For three weeks he chased Victorio, with only one encounter, in which the Apache held the high ground and were able to foil an attack by rolling rocks down on the troopers. Eventually, Morrow followed Victorio all the way into Mexico, but, now down to eighty-one soldiers and ten scouts, he called off the pursuit and returned to Fort Bayard on November 4, 1879.[24]

Victorio and his band remained safely in Mexico until January 1880, when he again raided into New Mexico. One more time the 9th Cavalry and other available units went into the field. During two months of cat and mouse there were four indecisive firefight, in which three of Morrow's men were killed and seven were wounded. One of the dead was Lt. James Hansell French.[25] These tactics continued until late February, when Colonel Hatch, taking personal field command, developed a plan to bring the renegades to bay. Victorio was believed to be in the San Andres Mountains, east of the Black Range and the Rio Grande. Major Morrow, with three companies of the 9th Cavalry, a detachment from the 15th Infantry, and several scouts, all reinforced by soldiers of the 6th Cavalry arriving from Arizona, would march into the mountains from the west. Captain Henry Carroll,[26] with four companies of the 9th Cavalry, would march from the east, and Captain Hooker, with three companies of the 9th

---

[24] Billington, pp. 92-93; William Leckie, pp.212-213.

[25] Heitman, p. 437. French, from Pennsylvania, graduated from West Point in 1874 and was immediately assigned to the 9th Cavalry.

[26] Heitman, p 286. Carroll joined the artillery as an enlisted man in 1859 and remained in that service until transferring to the cavalry in 1864. After the Civil War he was assigned to the 9th Cavalry upon it organization. He served as Brigadier General of Volunteers during the Spanish-American War and retired as Colonel of the 7th Cavalry in 1899.

Cavalry, a detachment of men from the 15th Infantry, and several Navajo scouts would attack from the north.[27]

Lieutenant Charles B. Gatewood, 6th Cavalry, was one of those officers from Arizona assigned to assist Hatch in his pursuit of Victorio. Gatewood, who would later gain fame as the man who convinced Geronimo to surrender wrote of the Victorio campaign "across the mountains and deserts of New Mexico. Up and down and across the valley of the Rio Grande, we followed Victorio for nearly a month, marching every day and often at night, on foot and horseback. The wary old fox (we gave him the credit, though he didn't deserve it) redoubled his watchfulness, particularly at night. Several times we almost had him, but he was too smart for us."[28]

On April 8, 1880, Carroll's column, seeking water more than a fight, encountered Victorio in Hembrillo Canyon.[29] Many of Carroll's men were ill from drinking gypsum laden water, and both men and horses needed the fresh water in the creek. An all night firefight ensued, which only ended when Captain Curwen B. McLellan's men from Morrow's command arrived on the scene to help drive the Apache from the water.[30]

---

[27] William Leckie, pp. 215-216.

[28] Gatewood, Charles B., "Campaigning Against Victorio in 1879," in Peter Cozzens (editor) *Eyewitnesses to the Indian Wars, 1865-1890: The Struggle for Apacheria,* Vol. I (Mechanicsburg, PA: Stackpole Books, 2001), p. 218. Kraft, Louis. *Gatewood and Geronimo* (Albuquerque: University of New Mexico Press, 2000). This is the story of Gatewood's southwestern adventures.

[29] Julyan, p. 164. Hembrillo Canyon is in the San Andres Mountains east of Hatch, New Mexico.

[30] Heitman, p. 676. McLellan, a native of Scotland, served in the Regular Army during the Civil War. Beginning as an enlisted man, he rose to the rank of Lt. Colonel in the 3rd Cavalry before retiring. He was cited for

Carroll was wounded in this engagement, as were several of his men, two of whom subsequently died. Victorio and some of his band escaped east to the Mescalero Reservation while others returned to the safety of Mexico.[31]

Realizing that many of the renegades were finding shelter and succor at the Mescalero Reservation, Hatch determined to disarm the Apache at the agency. Enlisting the aid of his old friend Colonel Benjamin Grierson and the 10th Cavalry in Texas, Hatch planned to meet on April 12. Grierson's report of his involvement in the New Mexico campaign contains the following description: "Telegraphic instructions from department headquarters directed me to proceed, without delay, with such force of cavalry as could be made available for the purpose to the Mescalero Agency, New Mexico, to assist in disarming the Mescalero Apache, the combination, with this objective in view, being already arranged by Generals Pope and Hatch to take effect on April 12, 1880, at which date it was desired that I should reach the agency from the southeast, with my troops, and report for orders."[32] With five companies of his 10th Cavalry and a detachment from the 25th Infantry, an aggregate of 280 men, Grierson arrived as ordered.

Victorio was now safely ensconced in Mexico, but a number of his followers from the pursuit through the San Andres Mountains, as well as many Mescalero warriors not willing to give up their weapons, were at

---

bravery several times, including the action at Hembrillo Canyon. His name is often misspelled as McClellan.

[31] Billington, pp. 93-94.

[32] Col. Benjamin Henry Grierson in the *Annual Report of the Secretary of War for the Year 1880* (Washington: Government Printing Office, 1880), p. 154.

the Agency when Hatch and Grierson arrived. The process of disarming the Indians did not begin until April 16, whereupon fighting broke out as some of the Apache tried to run. Grierson's troops gave chase, killing or wounding several Indians, but between thirty-five and fifty escaped to join Victorio. Patrolling through southeast New Mexico, Grierson returned to Texas, where he would soon encounter Victorio again.[33]

Of his time in New Mexico, Grierson wrote, "those who are so quick to censure, vilify, and abuse General Hatch and his hard-worked troops, officers and men, for not at once capturing or destroying Victorio and his band of marauders, do not stop to consider the great difficulties to be encountered in consummating this desired result. They seem to forget or are not aware of the nature or extent of the territory to be scouted over. The face of the high, dry table lands of New Mexico is broken here and there by ranges of rough and almost inaccessible mountains, and the Indians, with their minute and thorough knowledge of the country, throughout which there is a great scarcity of water, place the troops at great disadvantage."[34] Grierson and the 10th Cavalry would soon faced the same circumstances in West Texas.

Reinforced, Victorio crossed back into New Mexico in May. Word came to Sergeant George Jordan, Company K, 9th Cavalry, that the Apache were headed towards old Fort Tularosa, an abandoned post fifty miles west of Ojo Caliente. Because the post was abandoned, the small settlement was unprotected. A dispatch rider found Jordan and twenty-five men at a Barlow and Sanderson stage station. Night was coming on,

---

33 Robert Utley, *Frontier Regulars,* pp. 361-362.
34 Grierson, *Annual Report,* p. 157.

and it was a full day's march to the settlement; however, Jordan and his men set out in the dark, arriving at Fort Tularosa at six in the morning of May 14, 1880. Arriving first Jordan forted up and awaited events. Victorio was not long in coming, attacking in early evening, but was beaten off by the troopers. The Apache then turned their attention to the stock herd guarded by two soldiers and several teamsters. Jordan countered with an advance of ten of his men. The Indians were driven off with no loss to the herd or the troopers. Ten years later Jordan, a career soldier now serving as the First Sergeant of Company K, was awarded the Medal of Honor. Of the fight at the settlement at Fort Tularosa, Jordan stated that it "was short but exciting while it lasted."[35]

Returning from the Mescalero Reservation to Ojo Caliente, Hatch took time to refit. Both men and horses were worn out, and supplies were low. Still in the field on the trail of Victorio were Henry K. Parker, Chief of Scouts, and a contingent of his men. On May 23 at Palomas Creek Parker was able to engage the Apache, killing several and capturing seventy-five horses.[36] Out of ammunition and water, he chose not to pursue as Victorio moved towards Mexico. Hatch immediately sent Morrow in pursuit. On May 30 Morrow's men engaged Victorio's rear guard, killing three and wounding several. The pursuit continued to the border with Mexico, where the Army could not cross. However, six days later Morrow crossed paths with a small group of Apache moving south.

---

[35] Schubert, *Black Valor* pp. 74-76.

[36] Billington, p. 96; Dan Thrapp. *Encyclopedia of Frontier Biography*, vol. 3 (Lincoln: University of Nebraska Press, 1988), p. 1111-1112. Henry K. Parker, a native Texan, was a civilian appointed Chief of Scouts in 1879. Julyan, p. 257. Palomas Creek near Animas Creek on the east side of the Black Range flowed into the Rio Grande from the northwest.

In a sharp fight two Indians were killed and three wounded. One of the dead was Victorio's son.[37]

Of this entire campaign in New Mexico, General John Pope wrote, "the present is the fourth time within five years that Victorio's band has broken out. Three times they have been brought in and turned over by the military to the Indian Bureau authorities. Both Victorio and his band are resolved to die rather than go to the San Carlos Agency, and there is no doubt it will be necessary to kill or capture the whole tribe before present military operations can be closed successfully. The capture is not very probable, but the killing (cruel as it will be) can, I suppose, be done in time."[38] Beginning with the summer of 1880 circumstances and the theater of operations were about to change for both the Army and the Indians.

---

[37] William Leckie, p. 222.
[38] Pope, *Annual Report*, p. 88; Dan Thrapp. *Encyclopedia,* vol. 2, p. 1019. Morrow also commented on the New Mexico campaign, "I am heartily sick of this business. I have had eight engagements with the Victorio Indians and in each have driven and beaten them but there is no appreciable advantage...."

Chapter Five: The Victorio Campaign in West Texas: The Chase Ends

Colonel Grierson returned to Texas in late May 1880 to find that he was being ordered to send troops back to New Mexico amidst rumors that Victorio was once again going to cross over from Mexico. Grierson protested that this would leave West Texas unprotected. He also suspected that Victorio, rather than risk confronting troops in New Mexico again, would make his next move across the Rio Grande in Grierson's District of the Pecos. To counter the potential movement of his troops north, Grierson communicated with General Ord, commanding the Department of Texas, saying, "I telegraphed you June 24 that it would be more judicious to increase the force in the western part of the district of the Pecos, toward the Rio Grande and the Guadalupe Mountains, and thus have troops in position to be promptly concentrated to intercept and punish the marauders in case they attempted to cross into Texas, than to wear out troops in scouting northward into New Mexico."[1] Having witnessed the futility of having troops chase Victorio through New Mexico, Grierson determined to change tactics.

The first step was to bring force to bear where needed. Headquarters of the 10th Cavalry was Fort Concho, far removed from the proposed theater of operations. In May General Ord, to support Grierson, ordered headquarters and seven of the companies of the 24th Infantry from the Texas Valley to Forts Concho, Stockton and Davis. To facilitate

---

[1] Grierson, in the *Annual Report,* p. 159.

command in the field on July 10, Grierson left his headquarters at Fort
Concho for Fort Davis accompanied by Companies A, G and I and his
son Robert. Rather than fruitless pursuit, Grierson's plan was to guard the
Rio Grande crossings, the mountain passes and waterholes. The colonel
wrote that he "at once ordered Lieutenant Mills, Twenty-fourth Infantry,
then at Eagle Springs, in command of Pueblos, to throw his scouts out
along the Rio Grande to closely watch and report the approach of the
Indians; and I took the necessary measures to increase the force at Viejo
Pass, Eagle Springs, Quitman, and the Guadalupe's [sic], giving such
instruction to the officers in command as would ensure concert of action,
and prompt concentration of troops at any threatened point."[2]

To carry out his plan Grierson had immediately available eight
troops of the 10th Cavalry and four companies of the 24th Infantry to
protect river crossings from Viejo Pass to Quitman and beyond, numerous
waterholes, and the mountain passes. Four of Grierson's company
commanders, Captains Nicholas Nolan, Charles D. Viele, Thomas C.
Lebo, and Louis H. Carpenter, were original officers with the Tenth and
highly experienced. The active approach these officers and others took to
their task is illustrated by the record miles units from Fort Davis scouted

---

[2] Grierson, in the *Annual Report,* p.159; Frazer, pp. 157-158. Viejo Pass,
approximately twelve miles west of the present town of Valentine, is one of
the few places where the Sierra Viejo Mountains can be crossed from the Rio
Grande north of Presidio. Eagle Springs is southwest of Van Horn on the
north side of the Eagle Mountains, and Quitman refers to Fort Quitman
founded in 1858 on the Rio Grande approximately seventy miles down river
from El Paso. Abandoned during the Civil War, the fort was re-commissioned
after the War from 1868-1877. The Guadalupe Mountains straddle the
Texas-New Mexico border east of El Paso. Fort Davis maintained a sub-post
at Pine Springs, now the headquarters of Guadalupe Mountains National
Park.

in 1878, a total of 6,724. This effort paid dividends as the regiment gained an intimate knowledge of the country for which they were responsible in the coming campaign.[3]

In addition, Grierson could call upon the company of Texas Rangers based at Ysleta between El Paso and San Elizario. Commanded by Captain George W. Baylor, the Rangers were primarily charged with keeping the peace after a major conflict in late 1877 between the local Mexican population and Anglo commercial interests. This dispute was over the salt deposits at the base of the Guadalupe Mountains and came to be known as the El Paso Salt War. An uneasy peace prevailed, but the Rangers were on hand if trouble developed, and Baylor, especially, was anxious to chase Indians if the opportunity arose.[4] Also available for support was Company K, 8th Cavalry, stationed at Fort Davis, and the aforementioned contingent of Pueblo Scouts recruited from the El Paso area under the command of Lieutenant Frank H. Mills, 24th Infantry.

Mills and his scouts had already tangled with the Apache on June 11,1880 when he and several of his Pueblos, were attacked in Viejo Pass. Simon Olgin, the Pueblo chief, was killed.[5] Mills reported, "Shortly after

---

[3] Utley, *Frontier Regulars,* p. 362; Robert Utley, *Special Report on Fort Davis* (Santa Fe: National Park Service, 1960), pp. 72-73.

[4] Robinson, Charles H. III, *The Men Who Wear the Star: The Story of the Texas Rangers* (New York, Random House, 2000) pp. 224-231; p. 241. Gillett, James B., *Six Years with the Texas Rangers* (New Haven: Yale University Press, 1963), pp. 136-150, provides a personal account of the El Paso Salt War. Baylor's comment to Major John B. Jones, commander of the Frontier Battalion, was to ask "If he had any Indians out west that he wanted killed and scalped." Robinson, p. 241.

[5] Smith, *Old Army in Texas: A Research Guide to the U.S. Army in Nineteenth Century Texas* (Austin: Texas State Historical Association, 2000), p. 163; Ron Tyler (ed.), *The Handbook of Texas,* (Austin: Texas State Historical Association, 1996), pp. 495-496. These Pueblo scouts were Tigua

daylight, on the morning of the eleventh, while saddling to pursue the trail, my detachment was attacked by about 20 Indians, Apache. I ordered my detachment into the rocks and there made a stand, fighting about four hours. During the fight I sent a detachment to occupy a height commanding the position of the attacking Indians, and when these men opened fire the hostiles hastily retreated."[6] Mills, short of ammunition, collected the body of Olgin and retreated to Muerto Station.

Through his experiences during the Civil War, Grierson knew the value of communication during field operations and had with him a telegraph operator with a key and tools to cut into the line as needed. He also asked Lieutenant Charles Tingle, in charge of the military telegraph in Texas, to send an operator to Fort Quitman. On July 14 Grierson was informed that Colonel Adolpho Valle, with four hundred soldiers of the Mexican Army, had taken to the field in pursuit of Victorio. On July 18, informed that Valle was moving towards Quitman, Grierson, now at Fort Davis, determined to also march to that location.[7]

Grierson and his escort left Fort Davis on July 20, reaching Viejo Pass on July 21 and Eagle Springs on July 23. There he learned that Mexican advance forces had engaged Victorio's band and that both the Apache and the Mexican Army were moving towards Fort Quitman. Upon hearing this news Grierson wrote, "On the 27th I proceeded to

---

Indians, a tribe that followed the Spanish south after the Pueblo Revolt in northern New Mexico in 1680. They settled south of El Paso at Ysleta on the Rio Grande.

[6] Letter from the War Department to Congressman R.E. Thomason dated 1938 in Fort Davis National Historic Site file titled Viejo Pass. There is a 1936 Texas Centennial Historic Marker in Viejo Pass commemorating this fight.

[7] Utley, *Special Report*, p. 81; Grierson, in the *Annual Report*, p. 159.

Quitman: and on the 28th to my surprise the Mexican troops returned opposite that point entirely out of provisions, having exhausted whatever supplies they may have had not captured by Indians." The colonel had no choice but to assist his Mexican counterpart. "On account of their destitute condition, having had no food for three days, I furnished Colonel Valle, subject to approval of higher authority, one thousand pounds of flour, and eleven hundred and thirty pounds of grain."[8]

Grierson realized that the Mexican Army was no longer a viable force in the pursuit and that Victorio had no reason not to cross into Texas. On July 29 he left Quitman for Eagle Springs in an attempt to intercept Victorio somewhere north of the Rio Grande. In route, he was met by couriers from Captain John C. Gilmore, 24th Infantry, commanding at Eagle Springs. Gilmore's dispatch stated that Victorio had indeed crossed the river and was moving north. The officer bringing the news to Grierson was Lieutenant Henry O. Flipper, 10th Cavalry, the first African-American to graduate from West Point. Of his ride Flipper wrote, "Captain Nolan sent me and two men with dispatches to Gen. Grierson at Eagle Springs. I rode 98 miles in 22 hours mostly at night, through a country the Indians were expected to traverse in their efforts to get back to Mexico. I had no bad effects from the hard ride till I reached the General's tent. When I attempted to dismount, I found I was stiff and sore and fell from my horse to the ground, waking the general."[9] This ride was no mean feat in the harsh environment of West Texas.[10]

---

[8] Grierson, Annual *Report*, p. 159.
[9] Theodore Harris (ed.), *The Memoirs of Henry O. Flipper* (Fort Worth: TCU Press, 1997), p 34.
[10] Leckie, *Buffalo Soldiers*, p. 224.

Since he was already close to the waterhole in Quitman Canyon, the colonel determined to block Victorio's path, later writing, "Deeming it my duty, I camped directly in their line of march, and at the only water for a long distance north. I then had with me only First Lieutenant William H. Beck, Tenth Cavalry, one non-commissioned officer, and five privates – two of whom were teamsters – and my son Robert K. Grierson, who was *just* through school, was out in search of adventure and suddenly found it."[11] Grierson's small force fortified the waterhole in Quitman Canyon, called Tinaja de las Palmas, creating rudimentary stone breastworks.

Determined to bring as much force to bear as possible, Grierson sent word to Eagle Springs and Quitman by the east-and-west bound stagecoaches that passed during the night. At 1:00 am dispatch riders brought word that Victorio was encamped only ten miles south. Grierson sent these riders on to Quitman to ask that Captain Nolan and Company A march to his position quickly. Presuming Grierson to be in a desperate situation, the officers at Eagle Springs sent Lieutenant Leighton Finley and fifteen men from Company G to bring the colonel and his troops back to the safety of their camp. Of this misunderstanding Grierson said, "As I had no thought of being escorted there, or anywhere else, I immediately sent two of these men back with peremptory orders that all available cavalry be at once sent to my support. Being well supplied with ammunition, water, and provisions, I was confident of my ability to hold

____

[11] Ibid.

the position until their arrival, or so long as necessary."[12] At 9:00 a.m. on the morning of July 30, 1880, the Apache approached the waterhole.

Victorio's forces numbered approximately 150. Spying the entrenchments protecting the waterhole, he moved off to the east. Grierson promptly sent Lt. Finley and ten troopers to charge their position. The soldiers and Apache skirmished for the next hour, at which point Captain Charles Viele and Company C arrived from Eagle Springs. Initially mistaking Finley's men for the Indians, Viele's troopers opened fire forcing Finley back to the waterhole and the protection of Grierson's works. Some of Victorio's warriors set off in pursuit of Finley, while others turned to engage Viele. Both forces continued to exchange fire for the next hour.[13]

Within that hour, Captain Nicholas Nolan, Company A, arrived on the scene from Fort Quitman to the west. Some of the Apache then withdrew, and Viele was able to force his way through the rest to join Grierson. As Nolan approached, Grierson reported, "the Indians scattered and fled in great haste and confusion toward the Rio Grande, none having succeeded in going north." Grierson further noted, "We, undoubtedly, fought Victorio's whole effective force, and in the entire engagement, which lasted four hours, seven Indians were killed and a large number wounded. In the fight Lieut. S.R. Colladay, Tenth Cavalry, was wounded, and Private Davis, Company C, Tenth Cavalry, killed. Ten horses were killed and three horses and two mules wounded."[14] Grierson sent word to

---

[12] Grierson in the *Annual Report of the Secretary of War, 1880,* p. 160.
[13] Utley, *Special Report,* p. 83.
[14] Grierson in the *Annual Report,* p. 160.

Colonel Valle that Victorio was moving back towards Mexico, but the Mexican forces moved off in the opposite direction.[15]

Knowing that Victorio would try to cross again, Grierson increased his force at Eagle Springs and ordered Company E, 10th Cavalry from Fort Stockton and Company K, 8th Cavalry at Fort Davis to move west. He sent Company K, 10th Cavalry to scout through the Carrizzo Mountains and the Sierra Diablo. He also put the commander of the Pine Springs post in the Guadalupe Mountains on alert. On August 2 Victorio crossed the Rio Grande, engaging a cavalry patrol at Alamo Springs where one trooper was killed and one listed as missing. Grierson, with two companies, rode to Bass Canyon to intercept, but Victorio managed to avoid the screen of soldiers and moved north along the east side of the Sierra Diablo. The next possible water source was to the east of the Sierra Diablo at Rattlesnake Springs, and Grierson was determined to arrive there first.[16]

Victorio slipped the noose on August 4, 1880. Grierson soon received the news, saying later in his report, "I at once got my command in readiness and moved northwest, keeping a range of mountains between my command and the Indians, which effectually prevented their observing the movement. I left camp, ten miles nearly south of Van Horn's Station, at 3 o'clock a.m., the 5th, and reached Rattlesnake Springs at 11.45 p.m., making a march of sixty-five miles in less than twenty-one hours, without the loss of an animal, and found myself as I intended, in

---

[15] Utley, *Special Report*, p. 84.
[16] Grierson in the *Annual Report*, p. 160; Utley, *Special Report*, p. 84.

advance of the Indians."[17] As he had proved in his Vicksburg Raid, Grierson knew how to march men.

Captain Viele, commanding Companies C and G, 10th Cavalry, was dispatched to guard the waterhole. At 2:00 p.m. Victorio's warriors approached but were pushed back by volley fire from the troopers. Noticing that the water was actually protected by such a small force, the Apache approached a second time. At this juncture, Captain Louis Carpenter, commanding Companies B and H, 10th Cavalry, arrived and charged into the melee. The Indians scattered to the west. At approximately 4:00 p.m. a supply train approached from the southeast about eight miles away. Seizing the opportunity Victorio sent warriors to attack. The train was protected by Captain John Gilmore and Company H, 24th Infantry and a small detachment of cavalry. Gilmore deployed his men as skirmishers and "vigorously repulsed them, and compelled their rapid retreat, with the loss of one Indian killed and several wounded."[18]

Victorio's force then retreated into the Carrizzo Mountains to the south, with Captain Carpenter in pursuit. During the night small groups of Apache continued to try to reach the water of Rattlesnake Springs but they were repulsed. Of this fight Grierson reported, "It is impossible to tell the entire loss of the Indians, owing to the broken character of the country. Four are known to have been killed, and it is certain that many were wounded. A few ponies were captured. I am happy to state that in this engagement the troops suffered no loss."[19] Again, Grierson sent as many troops as possible in multiple directions to find Victorio.

---

[17] Ibid., p. 161.
[18] Grierson in the *Annual Report,* p. 161; Utley, *Special Report,* p 85.
[19] Grierson in the *Annual Report,* p. 161.

The Apache continued to be active in the area. Two days before the fight at Rattlesnake Springs, Captain William Kennedy, 10th Cavalry, and a patrol from the Pine Springs subpost in the Guadalupe Mountains were attacked near Bowen Springs, and a trooper was killed. Kennedy was subsequently able to pursue his attacker into the Sacramento Mountains, killing one warrior and one woman.[20]

On August 7, Captain Lebo arrived at Rattlesnake Springs and reported that on August 3 he had crossed the trail of a band of Apache moving down from the north to join Victorio. Grierson later wrote, "Captain Lebo, with Company K, Tenth Cavalry, arrived at 2 p.m., having carried out his instructions in a highly satisfactory manner. He thoroughly scouted through the mountains to Sulfur Springs, and struck a trail and followed it to the tops of the Sierra Diablo, where, on August 3d, he captured Victorio's supply camp, which consisted of about twenty-five head of cattle, a substitute for bread, made of the Maguay and other plants, berries, &c., and a large supply of beef on pack animals. He pursued the Indians, about fifteen in number, toward the Guadalupe Mountains, as far as Escondido Springs."[21] Grierson suspected that this was the same group that had encountered Kennedy the next day.

By the evening of August 7, the force at Rattlesnake Springs included Captain Viele with Companies C and G, Captain Lebo with Company K, and Captain Nolan with Company A. That evening Captain William Livermore with Company K, 8th Cavalry arrived. Livermore, an engineer, was scouting locations for a new fort in the region, and his 8th

----

20 Utley, *Special Report*, p. 85.
21 Grierson in the *Annaul Report*, p. 161.

Cavalry escort was under the command of Lieutenant John Pullman. On the morning of August 8th Grierson immediately put Pullman and his men to work, sending them to scout through Rattlesnake Canyon. That afternoon Captain Baylor and fifteen Rangers arrived in camp. With virtually his entire force in hand, Grierson developed a plan to find his elusive foe.[22]

Captain Carpenter was dispatched to guard Sulfur Springs, and Lieutenant Finley was sent to Apache Springs. Grierson with his headquarters party, Captain Gilmore and Company H, 24th Infantry, and Captain Livermore and his scouts, "climbed the rough and precipitous cliffs of the Sierra Diablo, two thousand feet high, and scouted over the mountains as far as practicable."[23]

On August 10, Captain Nolan and Company A, 10th Cavalry, Baylor and his Rangers, and Company K, 8th Cavalry were sent south through Fresno Canyon and then westward. Captain Gilmore was left at Rattlesnake Springs with Company H, 24th Infantry and Company K, 10th Cavalry. Grierson moved his headquarters party and Company C, 10th Cavalry to Sulfur Springs, where he sent Captain Carpenter around the west side of the mountains. In the meantime Captain Kennedy commander of forces in the Guadalupe Mountains was ordered to establish a blocking force should the Apache move north towards the Mescalero Reservation. Grierson later explained that, "The object of this disposition and movement of troops was to attack the Indians, from all sides, if found in the mountains, or if they were forced out, to find the

---

[22] Utley, pp. 85-86.
[23] Grierson in the *Annaul Report,* p. 161.

trail and pursue them. This caused Victorio and his band to move southward."[24]

The trail was discovered by Nolan and Carpenter on August 11, but Carpenter, with his horses exhausted from lack of water, had to withdraw. Nolan pursued the Apache all the way to the Rio Grande, where Victorio crossed into Mexico for the last time on the night of August 12, 1880. Before crossing and while making their escape his band attacked the east-bound stagecoach in Quitman Canyon. The driver, Ed Walde, turned his team back to Fort Quitman but his passenger, retired Union General James Byrne, the chief engineer for a Texas & Pacific Railroad survey, was killed.[25]

On August 18, Grierson sent Charles Berger, an interpreter and civilian scout, and several Indian scouts into Mexico to determine Victorio's location and intentions. At the same time Grierson began to move his forces back towards the Rio Grande at Fort Quitman, Ojo Caliente, and Eagle Springs. Captain Livermore and his 8th Cavalry escort were released to return to their prior assigned duty. Grierson established his headquarters at Eagle Springs, awaiting developments.[26]

Upon Berger's return, Grierson was able to report that "they found that the Indians were in a badly crippled condition, having their wounded with them, and their stock worn out, as an indication of which they were mostly on foot, driving their animals, avoiding their usual trails, passing over and skirting the roughest broken country. The Mexican troops had neither attacked them nor gotten in their way, but had given them open

---

[24] Ibid, p. 162.
[25] Gillett, *Six Years*, p. 181.
[26] Ibid.

passage westward."[27] With Victorio deep in Mexico on August 28th Grierson left the field for Fort Bliss at El Paso arriving there on September 1. For Colonel Grierson the Victorio campaign was over.

The 10th Cavalry was left with the job of holding the Rio Grande crossings and guarding waterholes while, in September, Colonel George Buell, 15th Infantry, with a mixed force of cavalry and infantry crossed into Chihuahua from New Mexico. Colonel Eugene Carr, 6th Cavalry crossed into Mexico from Arizona. They were to unite with a Mexican Army force of a thousand men under the command of Colonel Joaquin Terrazas and march on Victorio's stronghold in the Candelaria Mountains. Victorio had actually moved further south and Terrazas was uncomfortable with both the U.S. troops' being that far into in his country and the Army's use of Apache scouts. Terrazas, who was from an established and political family in Chihuahua City, also wanted sole credit for bringing Victorio to bay. He ordered Buell and Carr back across the border.[28]

On October 15, 1880, as the American force was returning to the border, Terrazas attacked Victorio's camp at Tres Castillos. Victorio was killed, along with sixty of his warriors and eighteen women and children. Two small groups were absent at the time, and one managed to find their way to the band of the Apache Chief Nana. Another group of approximately thirty-five crossed back into Texas and attacked a picket post of twelve men near Ojo Caliente, killing two. Captain Theodore

---

[27] Ibid.
[28] Utley, p. 364.

Baldwin, Company I, 10th Cavalry, chased them back into Mexico where they, too, eventually joined Nana.[29]

However, it would be the Texas Rangers who performed the last act of the Indian Wars in Texas. In early January 1881, a party of twelve warriors, four women, and four children stopped the stagecoach in Quitman Canyon, killing the driver and a passenger. In this instance Captain Baylor and the Rangers took up the pursuit, reinforced by Ranger Captain C.L. Nevill and his company stationed at Fort Davis. This combined force found the Indians camped in the Diablo Mountains on January 29. In the ensuing fight four men, two women, and two children were killed. The rest of the warriors fled north to New Mexico, but one of the women and two of the children were captured and taken to Fort Davis. The children were subsequently adopted by the post hospital steward, and the woman was later murdered by parties unknown. Baylor's was the last Indian fight in Texas.[30]

As the campaign came to a close, Grierson was extremely disappointed in the outcome, writing, "If the Mexican troops had been ready and in condition to attack the Indians when they were forced across the Rio Grande, or if I had had the authority to pursue them into Mexico, thus giving them no time to rest, there is little doubt that Victorio and his band would have been captured or destroyed." Regardless, he was extremely proud of his officers and men in the field, as well as the support units that made the campaign possible, thanking them in his final report. He was also clear about the problems his campaign faced, writing, "The

---

[29] Ibid.: For the exploits of Nana see Lekson, *Nana"s Raid.*
[30] Gillett, pp. 203-210; Utley, p. 88.

great difficulties to be encountered in operating against Indians in Western Texas, throughout which there is great scarcity of water, cannot be conceived by any one unacquainted with the nature and extent of the country."[31]

Summarizing the campaign, Grierson wrote, "By disposition made of my small force, the genuine pluck and earnest activity of the troops, Victorio and his bold marauders were three times headed off; twice whipped; driven from their stronghold in the Sierra Diablo; and twice forced back into Mexico."[32] However, the last word on the entire campaign from New Mexico to Texas should go to William Leckie: "The real victors were the buffalo soldiers of the Ninth and Tenth Cavalry. They had pursued and fought the great chief over thousands of blood-spattered miles in an unrelenting contest of courage, skill, endurance, and attrition."[33] While other problems, outlaws, and border troubles, would impact life in West Texas, the Indian Wars were over.

---

[31] Grierson in the *Annual Report,* p. 163.
[32] Ibid.
[33] William Leckie, p. 228.

Quitman Canyon (Diorama)
Diorama of Colonel Grierson, Robert, Lieutenant William Beck, and troopers fortifying the waterhole at Quitman Canyon in anticipation of the arrival of Victorio. (Courtesy Fort Davis National Historic Site)

Quitman Canyon: *Arrival of Reinforements* Original painting by Nick Eggenhoffer. *(Courtesy Fort Davis National Historic Site)*

Rattlesnake Springs, *Protecting the Supply Train* Original painting by Nick Eggenhoffer. *(Courtesy Fort Davis National Historic Site)*

Army Supply Train and Escort, Fort Davis c.1888
(Courtesy Fort Davis National Historic Site)

Sierra Diablo
(Courtesy Larry Francell)

Eagle Springs Historic Marker
(Courtesy Glen Ely)

The Journal of Robert Grierson

JOURNAL
Kept daily by
Robert Kirk Grierson
On the
Indian Chief Victorio War
Near Fort Davis 1880
The Personal narrative of a 19-year old Youth[1]

Camp Charlotte, Texas[2]

45 miles W. of Concho

Saturday July 10, 1880

Left Concho[3] this morning about 10:15. We started ¾ of an hour

sooner, but after going a piece beyond the graveyard had to go back after

Papa's hunting boots.

At Rock Creek the team that was sent out yesterday was hitched to

our ambulance, and we came on, getting here about 6:30 P.M. Cooper[4] in

---

[1] This is the title Barry Scobee gave to the Journal. Words or phrases in parentheses are Robert Grierson's. Words or phrases in brackets are added by the author to provide clarity.

[2] Camp Charlotte was a sub post of Fort Concho on the Overland Mail route at the Middle Concho River below Kiowa Creek in present northwestern Irion County. *Handbook of Texas*, Vol. I, p. 931; Haley, p. 156.

[3] Fort Concho, located at the confluence of the North and South Concho Rivers was established December 4, 1867 and abandoned June 20, 1889. The post is now an historic site within the city limits of San Angelo. Frazier, p. 147.

[4] Lt. Charles Cooper rose through the ranks, joined the 10th Cavalry on December 31, 1870. Robert may have the regiment wrong. No Cooper is found serving in the 24th Infantry. Heitman, p. 325.

charge of "K" Co. 24th Infantry, and Lt. Black[5] of that Co. left today – also Paymaster. Black is an operator – we brought him along in our ambulance after catching up with the Company; he stops at Grierson's Spring and we take the operator from there with us. Last part of the journey today was very dusty. Charlie[6] is well. Saw no game but rabbits and two flocks of quail. The camp is right on the hill – cool and breezy. Ate supper in tent – we threw in our lunch – things tasted good. Forgot to put in my journal the other day that Mrs. Smither[7] had a fine baby July 8th – Papa's birthday. We've been having a pleasant talk this eve. We've got a good supply of beer along – Mr. Millspaugh[8] gave us a doz. bottles and we had more than that before. I kissed Mrs.----------- "goodbye" this morning.

---

[5] Lt. William Black who began service as an enlisted man in the signal corps, was promoted to second lieutenant in the 24th Infantry, September 1879. He was a telegraph operator as well as a company officer. Heitman, p. 221.

[6] Lt. Charles Henry Grierson, West Point, assigned to the 10th Cavalry, June 1879, was Robert's older brother.

[7] Wife of First Lieutenant Robert Geno Smither, the 10th Cavalry Regimental Adjutant. He would serve with the regiment from its organization retiring as captain in 1888. Heitman, p. 905.

[8] L.J. Millspaugh was the Fort Concho post trader, or sutler. Of Millspaugh, J. Evetts Haley writes that he was "a small, dynamic, swashbuckling New Yorker possessed of more imaginative enterprise than practical execution. He was a hardy man who appreciated good music, loved the stage, and was a zestful actor in the spirited play of life which, for him, was a continual round of adventure." Haley, pp. 302-307. Over the years stationed at Fort Concho, Grierson had a sometimes friendly, sometimes stormy relationship with Millspaugh. Haley, pp. 302-307.

Grierson's Spring[9]

July 11, Sunday

It blew so last night that I lay awake for quite a while. Left Charlotte at 9 A. M. and got here at 4:30 P.M. Had a good talk with Charlie. Saw three antelope, soon after leaving camp. Passed a herd of 1,500 or more cattle. Road was very good today and not so dusty. Capt. Keyes[10] is well. Lieut. Black stays here and Operator McCarthy goes on with us. The spring and tank are to be walled up and enlarged soon. Capt. Keyes, Lt. Black, Papa and I took a look at the spring. It and tank are to be covered with flat rock. Papa got very close to a big rattlesnake on a hill near the spring. We killed it and Black has the rattles. Papa said it was 16 years old. Our wagon left here this morning. Catch it tomorrow. One of their mules foundered and had to be left here – Capt. Keyes gave 'em another to go on with. Showed my photos to Charlie and Lieut. Black last night.[11] There are three buildings with thatched roofs here and a stable looks quite military. Lieut. Black seems pleased with prospects; he will attend the

---

[9] Established by Lt. Mason Maxon, 10th Cavalry,and named after Col. Grierson the spring is located midway between Fort Concho and Fort Stockton and operated as a sub post of Concho. "Camp Grierson Springs," *Handbook of Texas Online*, Texas State Historical Association, (https:tshaonline.org/handbook/articles/qcc16).

[10] Lt. Alexander Scammel Brooks Keyes rose through the ranks of the Massachusetts Volunteers and was assigned to the 10th Cavalry in 1870. He was promoted to captain in 1873, retiring as major in the 3rd Cavalry in 1896. Heitman, p. 595.

[11] Robert had in his possession several photographs of girls he knew in Jacksonville and maybe Fort Concho. It is obvious from letters and comments from family and friends that the mothers of Jacksonville were consistently on the lookout for Robert. Shirley Leckie, p. 122-123, and Leckie and Leckie, pp. 255-56.

Telegraph Office here. 'John' who used to work for Gen. McLaughlen[12] is "striker" for Capt. Keyes.

Lower Escondida[13]

Monday, July 12.

All of us slept well last night. It rained before we went to bed, & some during the night. Left at 7:30 and got to Pecos [River] at 12 – watered and got here at 5:45. The wagon got here today at 1:30 P.M. Nothing had happened to them except they were fired upon by unknown parties, but when they returned the fire the others left – nobody on either side was hurt. No dust today. Rain extended here. We've had favorable weather so far – cool. The road from Spring to Pecos is [seems] new to me. The view is "immense" just before coming down into the Pecos valley. The road – a new cut – for 12 miles after crossing the river was rutty and rough, but with this exception it's been good. Tents are up and it looks quite camp like. A detachment from [Fort] Stockton is here on guard.

---

[12]Major Napoleon Bonaparte McLaughlen served as an enlisted man in the dragoons on the western frontier and rose through the ranks during the Civil War, being recognized for "gallant and meritorious" service at Chancellorsville, Gettysburg, and Fort Stedman, ending the War as Brigadier General of Volunteers. He was assigned to the 10th Cavalry, retired in 1882, and died in 1887. It was usual military etiquette to address officers by their Civil War rank. Heitman, pp. 674-75.

[13] Escondido Spring is approximately twenty-six miles west of the Pecos River and approximately twenty east of Fort Stockton and was described by Captain Samuel G. French as where "the water gushes out from beneath a shelf of rocks, and flows some distance down the creek. The county around is rocky and barren, covered with chaparral and prickly pear. The grazing is limited, and wood by no means plenty." *Reports of the Secretary of War, 1850*, (Washington Printing Office, 1850), p. 46. (Google Books)

Fort Stockton

Tuesday, July 13, 1880

Broke camp at 6:45 and got here at 11:15. Road very good. Papa telegraphed Mama. We're in camp back of hospital, and have run our own mess. Wiggins[14] is a good cook. All the officers in the post have been down to see us, and Papa is up in the garrison this eve. Both of us have had baths. Capt. Kelley[15], Lts. Hunt[16], Evans[17], Ripley[18],

---

[14] Randolph Wiggins joined the 10th Cavalry in 1869 and served after the Victorio Campaign as cook. He then settled in Fort Davis and was the teacher at the first African-American school organized in Fort Davis, 1888. Lucy Jacobson and Mildred Nored, *Jeff Davis County, Texas* (Fort Davis, TX: Fort Davis Historical Society), p. 109 and 303.

[15] Capt. Joseph Morgan Kelley was another officer who rose through the ranks in the Civil War. He stayed in the Army, and was originally assigned to the 38th Infantry (an African-American regiment that was combined with the 41st Regiment to create the 24th Infantry) and transferred to the 10th Cavalry in 1870. He retired with the rank of major in 1898. Heitman, p. 588.

[16] Lt. Levi Pettibone Hunt, West Point, 1870, was assigned to the 10th Cavalry upon graduation, and served with the regiment until 1901. Heitman, p. 556.

[17] Lt. George Howard Evans, West Point, 1872, spent his entire career with the 10th Cavalry, retiring as captain in 1898. Heitman, p. 409.

[18] Lt. Henry Lewis Ripley, an enlisted man in the Engineers, was promoted from the ranks to Second Lieutenant in the 24th Infantry in 1879, rising to the rank of major in the 8th Cavalry. Heitman, p. 832.

Maj. O'Beirne[19] and Capt. Armes[20] have been here. I saw Mr. Corbett[21] –
expected to see Frank this eve, but I guess he'll not be in from the ranche.
Papa has got two horses to take along. Rode on to Corbett's store this eve.
Strike out for Davis in the morning. I read this afternoon. It is getting to
be fine moonlight. How I'd like to be in J'ville [Jacksonville, Illinois] this
eve.

"Hackberry Creek" (mudhole)

Wednesday, July 14, '80

McCarthy and I had a bath in the bathhouse before breakfast. Saw all of
the officers and Mrs. Baldridge, the Chaplain, Mrs. Colladay, Mrs.
Baldwin and another lady at Chaplain's; also Mrs. Nolan & Katie[22] – a
few days ago their home was struck by lightening, but no one was hurt –
shingles were ripped off, holes torn in the roof, a stovepipe cut as with a

---

[19] Maj. Richard Fitzgerald O'Beirne, a native of Canada, served as an officer
with the Michigan volunteer infantry during the Civil War and was
recognized for his service at North Anna and the Overland Campaign.
Electing to stay in the Army, first with the 32nd Infantry and then the 21st
Infantry, he was promoted to major in 1879 and assigned to the 4th Infantry.
He finished his career as Lieutenant-Colonel of the 15th Infantry, and died in
1991. Heitman, p. 755.

[20] Capt. George Augustus Armes, an enlisted man in the Civil War, was
recognized for his service, including Hatcher's Run, was one of the 10th
Cavalry's senior company officers and retired from service in 1883. Heitman,
p. 169.

[21] M. F. Corbett was the post trader (sutler) and local merchant. He sold
Pecos County the block where the courthouse was built. James Collett, *Fort
Stockton*, (Charleston, South Carolina: Arcadia Publishing, 2011), p. 25. The
most comprehensive history of Fort Stockton is Clayton W. Williams, *Texas'
Last Frontier: Fort Stockton and the Trans-Pecos, 1861-1895* (College
Station: Texas A&M Press, 1982).

[22] Benjamin Logan Baldridge was the Fort Stockton Army Chaplin. Heitman,
p. 185. The other ladies Robert lists were wives of company officers. Katie is
unknown but, likely, the daughter of one of the officers.

knife, plastering knocked off, etc. Had a spring on ambulance tightened. Left about 10 – Leon Holes at 12 & here at 4:15. There was enough water here for stock. I read a lot in "Good-for-nothing" this afternoon after getting to camp. Met 4 men today (soldiers) after a deserter from [Fort] Davis. Belonged to "C" Co. We are 35 mi. from Stockton. I hope there will be some mail at Davis for me. We'll be there several days. I am going to try to learn telegraphy from the operator. Will try and get an old "key" at Davis.

Fort Davis, Texas

Thursday, July 15

Left camp at 6:45; got to Barilla [Springs] at 10, & here at 5 P.M. We waited before getting to Point of Rocks for the wagon over an hour, but it didn't come in sight, & has not got here yet – will be tomorrow. Serenaded us this eve. Both of us have taken baths. Occupy [Capt. Louis] Carpenter's[23] quarters – he is in the field. Took dinner and will mess with

---

[23] Capt. Carpenter, born in New Jersey, was a graduate of the University of Pennsylvania joining the Union Army as a private. Winning honors at Gettysburg and Winchester, Virginia, he ended the war as Colonel of the 5th United States Colored Cavalry. One of the original company officers of the 10th Cavalry, he was awarded the Medal of Honor for riding to the rescue of Major George Forsyth, who was besieged by Cheyenne, Arapaho and Sioux on the Republican River (Beecher Island) in eastern Colorado, September 1868. He retired in a brigadier-general in 1899, having served as a division commander in the Spanish-American War. Heitman, p 284; Thrapp, *Encyclopedia,* vol. 1, p. 229.

Woodward,[24],McLaughlen and Lebo's[25] mess. Most of the officers called here this evening. Nothing in the mail.

Friday, July 16, 1880

Slept on the lounge last night – didn't wake up once during the night. Wagon got in about 7 o'clock this morning. I was over at reading room after breakfast. Before this I shaved myself at Maj. Woodward's – am letting my mustache grow. After coming back from reading room I read [illegible] and finished all but a few pages. After dinner Papa, Maj. Woodward, Gen, McLaughlen, Lt. Black, and I went out to camp.7m,

[24] Lt. Samuel Lippincott Woodward joined the 6th Illinois Cavalry as a private in 1862. He was on the raid through Mississippi and impressed Grierson, who promoted him to staff. After the War he joined the 10th Cavalry, where he served Grierson with dedication until Grierson's retirement. Heitman, p. 1059; Leckie and Leckie, p. 73.
[25] Thomas Coverly Lebo served with the Pennsylvania Cavalry during the Civil War and joined the 10th Cavalry as a First Lieutenant at the time of the regiment organization. Heitman, p. 623. During his service with the Tenth he was mentioned three times in General Orders for "good judgement, energy and conspicuous gallantry in action with Indians." He was one of Grierson's best company officers, and as a major in the 6th Cavalry, he led the regiment up San Juan Hill, Cuba. He retired a Brigadier General in 1905. Thrapp, *Encyclopedia*, vol. 2, p. 827.

South East. Captains Nolan,[26] Baldwin,[27] Lts. Colladay,[28] Flipper,[29] and Jouett[30] are there.

The camp is in a wide place of the canyon, and it is one of the most picturesque places I ever saw – rocky and abrupt hills (here and there with canyons between them) in every direction.[31] All well at camp. After getting back I finished my 'dutch book.' Will read something from Tick next. Had a shower this afternoon. Papa leaves Monday or Tuesday.

---

[26] Captain Nicholas Nolan was one of the original company officers. An immigrant from Ireland, he joined the artillery in 1852, transferring to the 2nd Dragoons in 1858. He served in the cavalry during the Civil War. In 1877 he led a patrol onto the Staked Plains of Texas where, in the heat of summer, he found himself eighty-six hours without water, almost losing his command. He was promoted to major in the 3rd Cavalry in December 1882 but died the next year. Heitman, p. 750; Thrapp, *Encyclopedia*, vol. 2, p. 1059.

[27] Captain Theodore Anderson Baldwin joined the 10th Cavalry in 1870 and served as brigadier general of volunteers during the Spanish-American War and Colonel of the 7th Cavalry before retiring as Brigadier General in the Regular Army in 1903. Heitman, p. 186.

[28] Samuel Rakestraw Colladay served in the Pennsylvania Cavalry during the Civil War and joined the 10th Cavalry in 1867. He was wounded at the fight at Tinaja de las Palmas and died in 1884, likely in part from complications from that wound. Heitman, p. 317.

[29] Henry Ossian Flipper was the first African-American graduate of West Point. Assigned to Nicholas Nolan's Company A of the 10th Cavalry, he distinguished himself during the Victorio Campaign, with Grierson writing, "I can testify to his efficiency and gallantry in the field. He has repeatedly been selected for special and important duties, and discharged them faithfully and in a highly satisfactorily manner." He was later court-martialed and dismissed from service. As a civilian he became a successful surveyor and mining engineer. In 1976 the wrongful sentence was changed, and he was granted a posthumous honorable discharge, and on February 19, 1999, President Bill Clinton granted a full pardon. Heitman, 425; Thrapp, *Encyclopedia*, vol. 1, pp. 501-502.

[30] James Stockett Jouett joined the 10th Cavalry in 1877 and resigned from service in 1889. Heitman, p. 584.

[31] Fort Davis, founded in 1854, is located at the mouth of a box canyon bounded by Sleeping Lion Mountain to the south and North Ridge to the north, both of which shelter what is now called Hospital Canyon.

Before getting to camp there is Schooley's[32] graded road about $1^1/_4$ mile long descending into the Cañon; it is a fine work – it is evenly graded enough for a Rail Road. Very cool here.

Saturday, July 17, '80

Wrote to Mama this forenoon. Read in Tick's [illegible] today. This afternoon I was at telegraph office and all around the Q.M.D. [Quartermaster's Department] with Maj. Woodward. Have a very good stables here. It rained some today – they have had an unusual amount of rain lately. There is a ball this eve at the Reading Room, for Papa. He has gone but I always feel out of place at a "hop," and anyhow I have nothing to wear – I'd rather go anywhere else. I don't feel very well. We leave Monday and I shall not feel a bit sorry.

It is delightful moonlight – 'my thoughts are far away.'

Sunday, July 18 '80

I didn't sleep well last night. I dreamed – thought that a horse and buggy ran away with Mama and hurt her awfully. I woke up frightened and exhausted. I had a stomach ache this morning. Maj. Woodward gave me some whiskey, and I've felt better. Made out a list of commissary things to be gotten, and took inventory of what we have. Papa rec'd word

---

[32] Capt. Davis Schooley, 25th Infantry, was assigned the task of improving the road through Musquiz Canyon southeast of Fort Davis. Chaplin George Mullins commented that, "the labor was herculean and the work accomplished positively wonderful." Jacobson and Nored, p. 75.

that the Indians are moving towards Eagle Pass.[33] The three companies in camp, and Capt. Lebo's start for the field tomorrow. We will be very apt to start too. Gen. McLaughlen and I climbed the hill South of the parade this afternoon after dinner. The view is fine. I was up on it, and the one North of the parade 2 years ago. I came down an almost perpendicular place this afternoon. I finished "Red Riding Hood" in German and read most of [illegible] today.

There will be four in our mess – Papa, Beck, Operator & I – wish to thunder I could be of some good. You bet I'll perform anything to the best of my ability that I'm called on to do. I should like to see an Indian fight. Papa got a letter from Mama this morning – all well. Paymaster came today, and the troops which start into the field tomorrow have been paid already.

Monday, July 19th 1880

I finished [illegible] this morning before breakfast. Got commissaries, etc. today and are all ready to start in the morning. Troops got off today. Wrote to Mama & to Aunt Louisa,[34] and Papa wrote to Uncle John[35] today. Be glad when we get away.

---

[33] Eagle Springs, approximately half way between Van Horn and Fort Quitman was a central location and often Grierson's main base of operations during the campaign.

[34] Louisa Semple was Grierson's outspoken sister who was often a member of the household. She once wrote Alice that "the idea of the family of a Post Commander being made the servants of a whole regiment of shiftless things, is simply disgusting and intolerable and it is time one should try to make them perceive it." Shirley Leckie, *Colonel's Lady*, p. 66.

[35] John was Grierson's older brother. Of a speculative nature, he often relied on his younger brother to provide financial assistance.

Gen McLaughlen has his ditch nearly done. It is to prevent the water from rushing through the post during a hard rain.[36]

Wednesday, July 21st 1880

Left Davis yesterday at about 11:45. We called at Murphey's – there are 3 or four young ladies there.[37] We put up a telegraph pole at Point of Rocks.[38] Capt. Lebo camped at Crow's Nest.[39] Five wagons from Carpenter's camp, and the returning telegraph repairing [crew] were also camped there. We took lunch, and waited till Captain Lebo came. Got to El Muerto (35m) about 8 o'clock.[40] Captains Baldwin, Nolan, and Lt. Colladay were camped there. Lt. Beck[41] stopped with Colladay, I with Baldwin, and Papa with Nolan. Wagon didn't get in till after 10 p.m. I

---

[36] Fort Davis, built at the mouth of Hospital Canyon, had a tendency to flood during rare but periodically heavy rains. In order to mitigate the problem ditches were dug by the soldiers to both the south and the north of the officers' line to provide drainage. Today, as one enters the fort, he or she passes over a bridge that crosses the south ditch.

[37] Daniel Murphy arrived in the area before the Civil War and operated a saloon. Weathering the storms of war, he became one of the leading citizens of Fort Davis as a merchant, rancher, and freighter. Wooster, p. 55; Jacobson and Nored, pp. 355-357.

[38] A large, rocky formation, Point of Rocks is approximately twelve miles west of Fort Davis on State Highway 166, and is currently a favorite picnic area.

[39] Crow's Nest is a water source approximately seven miles past Point of Rocks on Highway 166, and is currently a small subdivision of homes.

[40] El Muerto Station was a stagecoach stop created before the Civil War that continued into the post-War period. Since the road to El Paso followed water sources, as opposed to the modern highway system, El Muerto is not now accessible but was approximately thirty-five miles west of Fort Davis.

[41] Lt. William H. Beck had served with Grierson since 1862, joining the Illinois Cavalry as an enlisted man. He served as Grierson's adjutant during the campaign and often used Robert as his assistant. He served in the Spanish-American War as Colonel of the 49th Volunteer Infantry, ending his career as Lt. Col. of the 3rd Cavalry.

didn't have chance to write [in] journal last night. Lebo is ordered to Fresno,[42] Baldwin is on his way here, Carpenter's camp Viejo Pass,[43] Capt. Nolan to Quitman, and Lt. Colladay to Eagle Springs. We left El Muerto at 1:50 P.M. today, and got here at 7:45. We are all mounted and have an escort of 2 sergeants and 11 men. Captain Baldwin camped at a pool about 8 m. this side of El Muerto. There have been heavy rains – plenty of water & grass, but saw no game at all. I lugged the Winchester. Our outfit goes to the "9 m. hole" beyond El Muerto tomorrow, and we will meet there tomorrow. We could see Guadalupe Peak[44] today. Captain Carpenter is all well. I did a good deal of copying for Lt. Beck this morning. I feel pretty tired – 35 miles is considerable for the first time. It is cool & cloudy though. Rained very hard around us, and we got a few sprinkles. Some of Colladay's men were dismounted yesterday as horses had sore backs – guess they're arranged to let 'em ride in wagons. Well I must get to bed early.

---

[42] Fresno Canyon, at the southern end of the Sierra Diablo Mountains, was a source of water. In keeping with his plan to keep Victorio away from water sources Grierson wanted a military presence there. William Leckie, p. 227.

[43] Vieja Pass is easily accessible to Mexico through the Sierra Vieja Mountains. It also includes a permanent spring. The location was deemed so important that during the border troubles with Mexico in the early 20th Century the Army constructed a Quartermaster's Depot, Camp Holland, and garrisoned troops there. On May 12, 1880, Lt. Frank Halsey Mills and a detachment of Pueblo Indian Scouts were attacked in Vieja Pass, and the chief scout and tribal leader, Simon Olguin, was killed. Wooster, p. 102. During the campaign the 10th Cavalry maintained a supply depot there. Today the spring is still a good source of water, and the and the ruins of Camp Holland are in private hands. Mills was in command of the Pueblo Scouts. After the fight at Viejo Pass he moved to Eagle Springs. He would remain with the 24th Infantry until retirement in 1892. Heitman, p. 713.

[44] Guadalupe Peak is the highest point in Texas but overshadowed by its headland, El Capitan, a remnant Permian Period reef. Fort Davis maintained a sub-post there at Pine Springs.

"Nine Mile Water Hole"

Thursday, July 22nd 1880

I slept in Dr. McLoon's[45] tent on the ground, Papa put up at "Hotel Carpenter," and Lt. Beck with Lt. Ayres. I slept bully and guess the rest did. After breakfast papa, Ayres, Dr. & I mounted, we went up the cañon to Viejo Spring. Saw the site of Mills fight with the Indians, but saw no Indians by a damn sight. The scenery is fine. Capt. Carpenter has a few men stationed on a high point near the spring, and they can see clear into Mexico. Left camp at 12 & got here at 4:30. Rained all the time we were on the way but a few minutes. I got soaking wet to the skin. Changed everything but my boots – took a sponge bath & had one of the men rub me dry. I ride a bay horse of Lt. Beck's – it frets a good deal and can't walk fast, so that I had to trot nearly all the way, and it was anything but comfortable. If my posteriors were not of the best quality they certainly'd've been sore. Have felt fine since supper and with my dry things on. Lt. Colladay is camped here also. Mr. McCarthy "cut in" here, and rev'd telegrams for Papa and sent a number this eve'. They have changed the boundaries of the Districts so that Pena Colorado comes under Shafter. Papa telegraphed that he thought it should be left in his district as a wintering place for troops.[46] We came some distance out of

---

45 Dr. Eugene McLoon graduated from the University of Pennsylvania School of Medicine and served at Fort Davis as a civilian contract surgeon in 1880. Donna Smith, *List of Physicians and Surgeons Who Served at Fort Davis* (Fort Davis National Historic Site, unpublished file).
46 Brigadier General Edward O.C. Ord was commander of the Department of Texas, while Grierson was commander of the District of the Pecos. Colonel William Shafter, 1st Infantry, was responsible for the District of the Bravo. Charged with building a new military road from the Devil's River to Camp Pena Colorado (near present Marathon, Texas), a sub-post of Fort Davis, Ord

the way today, but made good time as it was – considerably over 20m. (25 I'm pretty certain.) in $4^1/_2$ h. We saw some quail, a jackassrabbit, and a number of deer tracks.

Papa rec'd a dispatch this eve' saying Lt. Davis[47] had a daughter – "Rah" for them. We'll go to Eagle Springs tomorrow – over 50 miles. Well I feel as if I could sleep. Adieu.

Friday July 23rd 80

McCarthy sent some dispatches & I helped him fix the line. Colladay got off early, and our wagon left somewhat before we did. We got off at 9 o'clock. Watered at Van Horn's[48] well and got here – Nolan's Camp at 8:30. Captain Gilmore[49] & operator were on a stage for West today. Lt. Mills (in command of Indian scouts) was here this evening – is stationed here. Revd. news that Victorio with 60 warriors & lots of horses and cattle is in Mexico, 40 miles from here. Rio Grande is up so that they can't cross. I guess we'll nab him when the river is low enough for him to

extended Shafter's district. *Annual Report of the Secretary of War, 1880, p. 111.*

[47] Lt. William Davis, Jr., joined the 10th Cavalry in 1867 and at this time was serving a regimental quartermaster. He retired from service as a captain in 1897. Heitman, p. 360.

[48] Van Horne's Well is approximately twelve miles south of the town of Van Horn, the seat of Culbertson County, and named for Major Jefferson Van Horne, 3rd Infantry, who passed through the area in 1849 taking troops and supplies to El Paso. Glen Sample Ely, *The Texas Frontier and the Butterfield Overland Mail 1858-1861* (Norman: University of Oklahoma Press, 2016) p. 287.

[49] Capt. John Curtis Gilmore, a Medal of Honor winner, joined the 24th Infantry in 1869. Captain of Company H, he was in command at Eagle Springs. He won the Medal of Honor for distinguished conduct in the Battle of Salem Heights, Virginia, May 3, 1863 seizing the colors of his regiment and gallantly rallying his men under a very severe fire of the enemy while serving as major, 16th New York Infantry. Heitman, p. 458.

cross. Papa is going to apply for permission to cross into Mexico. Supper before 10 this eve.' Try to write more tomorrow night.

Saturday, July 24th 80

We are still at Eagle Springs. Colladay got in at 7:30. Took breakfast with us. Papa was pretty sick this forenoon – stomach out of order – he worked like a horse though sending telegrams. I copied nearly a doz. today. Communicated with [Fort] Quitman.[50] Papa sent a couple of Pueblo Scouts from Quitman to the Mexican Commander. Saw Lt. Dodge[51] of Col. Gilmore's Co. today.

Most of Colladay's & Nolan's wagons went back to Davis for supplies. I sent a congratulatory telegram to Mama (about Lt. Davis). Operator worked like a "hoss" today. Came 50 miles yesterday.

Sunday, July 25th 80

Lt. Read[52] & escort came from Fresno today – hardly any water, and Captain Lebo leaves tomorrow for water hole 15m. from Muerto where some of his forage was left.

We were going to start to Quitman today but didn't – have moved to telegraph line ½ mile from former camp. Could get no messages

---

[50] Fort Quitman is approximately seventy miles south of El Paso on the Rio Grande. Established September 28, 1858, to protect the overland trail, the post was named for Major General John Quitman, hero of the Mexican War. By the time of the Victorio Campaign it was no longer an active fort but was manned as needed by Grierson. Frazer, pp. 157-158.

[51] Lt. Charles Dodge rose from the enlisted ranks to second lieutenant in the 24th Infantry where he served until his death in1898. Heitmen, p. 376.

[52] Lt. Robert Doddridge Read, West Point, was assigned to the 10th Cavalry in June 1877. He remained with the regiment, achieving the rank of major in 1903. Heitman, p. 819.

through today – line must be down. Don't know where we'll go tomorrow. Papa, Lt. Beck & I went to camp the eve.' Studied some Spanish today.

Monday, July 26th 1880

Waited for the line to work today, so didn't get off anywhere; it is down between here and Davis – got one message from Bliss.[53] Mail got in in the middle of the night. This morning Papa told me there were three letters for me; one was from mama, one from Will McLaughlen, and the other from Emilie Miller with a card photo. Tell you I was glad to get these letters. Papa recd. a communication by courier from Gen. Valle,[54] Commander of Mexican forces – it was in Spanish – also a translation with it. Lt. Beck and I understood most of it without looking up any words. Did quite a little copying today. Copied the Mexican dispatch among the number. Wrote to Mama this afternoon. Papa read my letter & although there were some "sentimentalities" (in referring to the letters I recd.) in it, he said nothing except, "Your letter is all right." I went some distance away, however, while he read it. Studied some Spanish today. Captain Nolan, Lt. Colladay, Lt. Mills & Capt. Gilmore visited us today. I

---

[53] Fort Bliss, established June 24, 1851, by Capt. Jefferson Van Horne, 3rd Infantry, was named for Capt. William Wallace Smith Bliss, General Zachary Taylor's son-in-law. The post, adjacent to El Paso, was moved and abandoned and reactivated several times and is still active. Frazer, pp. 143-144.

[54] Adolpho Valle, whose actual rank in the regular Mexican Army was colonel, notified Grierson by telegraph on July 18 that Victorio was moving north to Texas. To that point Grierson did not know the location of the Apache.

went with Johnson[55] and RobertYoson[56] up to the spring in the ambulance to water just before supper.

Lt. Read & a detachment came from Carizzos[57] yesterday, and left for "15 mile water hole" (from Muerto) this morning. As there is little water at Fresno, Lebo has returned to the above point. If we stay here tomorrow I think I'll take a hunt in the mts. Some bighorn and blacktails have been seen lately. In letter to Mama I said: "Emilie enclosed a card photograph, as I requested, and since the receipt of her cordial & interesting letter I have experienced a "peculiar exhilaration." I was agreeably surprised to get Will's letter – it is a good thing to be on the 'good side of the family.'

Nothing in this eve's mail for me, but I think I'll get more letters soon. This evening the men had "bear grass cabbage," "chaparral," and "joint tea" for supper. This prairie cabbage (big bulb that grows at the bottom of the grass like an onion) is a new thing. It tasted like boiled cabbage when cooked up with bacon.[58]

---

[55] There were sixteen enlisted men named Johnson serving with the 10th Cavalry in the summer of 1880. None particularly stands out as the man to whom Robert refers. Charles Johnson served with the regiment from its formation and is listed as a blacksmith, and this may have been a skill that Grierson thought he needed. *Roster of Men Serving at Fort Davis*, Binder on File at Fort Davis National Historic Site.

[56] Robert J. Robertson was a corporal and listed as company clerk, and he is the most likely of the three Robertsons serving with the 10th Cavalry in 1880. Ibid.

[57] Carrizzo Spring, north of present day Van Horn, is at the east end of Fresno Canyon and the south end of the Sierra Diablo. It was one of the water sources that Grierson determined to protect should Victorio try to break north.

[58] "Bear grass is one common name for any one of numerus species of *Nolina* possibly better known in this area as sacahuista. However, *Nolina* species are poisonous. The bear grass reference may be to a species of *Dasylirion* sotol, which resembles bear grass. Today *D. leiophyllum* (smooth sotol)

Fort Quitman (what's left of it.)

Tuesday, July 27, 1880

Line wouldn't work this morning. Left at 10:15 and got here about 5:30 after a pleasant ride. We passed through quite a shower & there was lots of rain around us. We had a detachment. Captain Nolan's Co. left today from this point. Mr. Palmer, the tall young operator is a mighty nice young fellow. He and I went in swimming in the Rio Grande (about 150 yards from here) this eve.' Mail came in at 10:00 P.M. He got a letter from his wife – has been married about three months. Lt. Beck got a letter from his wife – extent of mail for our party. Papa had hired a Mr. Berger[59] as scout – he is French – speaks also German & Mexican and some Italian. I've had fun talking German with him. He and some Pueblos will probably go to Col. Valle's forces soon; wish I could go. This afternoon Papa and I right after getting here went up to the old post & examined it.

---

occurs in the Eagle Springs vicinity. And we know that Native Americans and early Europeans ate baked sotol 'hearts' (the basal stem with leaves removed). Sotol hearts covered by leaf bases could have been described as cabbage. 'Joint tea' is commonly called Mormon Tea. Two species of Mormon Tea occur in the vicinity of Eagle Springs: *Ephedra aspera* and *E. trifurca*. Today the term 'chaparral' is applied to thickets of a wide array of hard-leafed species, occurring at mid-mountain elevations. I can't imagine chaparral shrubs being eaten." Email from Dr. Michael Powell, Emeritus Professor of Biology and Director of the Herbarium Sul Ross State University, February 10, 2017. The word chaparral is also a common name for the road runner, a member of the cuckoo family, not generally known as a food source. Email from Kelly Bryan, retired Texas Parks & Wildlife Naturalist, April 7, 2017.

[59] Charles Berger, a well respected civilian scout for the Army, became a subject of the court-martial of Henry Flipper when, in December 1880, he applied for leave and requested the use of a government owned horse. Flipper, as acting post quartermaster, supplied the animal and Berger promptly disappeared. Charles H. Robinson, *The Court Martial of Lieutenant Henry Flipper* (El Paso: University of Texas at El Paso Press, 1994), pp. 11-12.

Some of the quarters are still pretty good, though the windows and doors are of course all gone. It is refreshing to see cottonwood trees. I enjoyed my bath & waded over into Mexico. Try and write something better tomorrow evening. Thirty five miles today.

Quitman

Wednesday, July 28 '80

Laid over here today. Col. Valle's part of the army has a large amount of provisions captured by the Indians (from a train), & being half played out returned here today. Papa sent to Captain Nolan & got 3 sacks of corn, 2 of oats & 5 of flour for the Mexicans. Johnson brought it to the river bank, and the Mexicans ferried it over in a sort of a raft. I went down to Captain Nolan's camp in the ambulance. He got in about noon, & and is camped about a mile below on the river at good grass. One Mexican officer (Captain) came over this forenoon, and this afternoon Col Valle, another Captain, and a friend of Col. Valle's came over on the raft after the first load of grain was taken over. We had a heavy rain this afternoon, and had to move camp to higher ground nearer the adobe house, (used as telegraph office & quarters for detachment). The officers have dined and supped with us, and will stay all night, as the river is too dangerous to cross, particularly at night – it has been rising some too. Col. Valle & his friend invited me to go to Chihuahua[60] and visit them – bet I will if I get half a chance – they say there are lots of pretty senoritas there.

---

[60] Chihuahua City, capitol of the State of Chihuahua which shares a border with west Texas along the Rio Grande.

I spoke a good deal of German (with Mr. Berger) some French and exhausted my Spanish; talked foreign whenever I could. Col Valle speaks French and one of his captains also. Perhaps we will return to Eagle Springs tomorrow. But I hope not. You bet I made use of Mr. Berger. As the soldados Mexicanos came here we did not have to send any couriers. I vomited up everything I've eaten for a week (judging from the amount) soon after supper, and have felt first rate ever since.

Presented of Col. Valle

3 bottles of beer	1lb. butter
1 bottle of Lemon Sugar	1 lb. coffee
1 can beef	1 pt. pickles
1 can corn	2 lbs. sugar
1 can peas	pepper& salt
1 can peaches	bread, 4 lbs. flour
1 can damsons[61]	$^{1}/_{2}$ box crackers

Names of the Mexicans entertained at Fort Quitman, Tex. July 28-29 '80. by Gen. Grierson. Languages spoken by each.

Colonel Adolfo T. Valle – Fr. Sp.

Captain Laurino R. Valdes – Sp.

Captain Antonio Lestrade – Fr. Sp.

Senor Don Juan Terrazas, Nephew of Ex. Gov. Terrazas of Chihuahua – Sp.

Eng.

---

[61] Plums

In camp at waterhole 12 or 15 miles West of Eagle Springs
on the Quitman Road.

Thursday, July 29th, 1880

The officers slept well and looked better today than yesterday. Line still out of fix. Officers crossed back into Mexico in the forenoon. We left at 1:30 and got here at 7:15. In the canyon. Young[62] & two other men (soldiers) saw a man on top of a ridge about ½ mile off. He and the men went after him, and they shot twice and made the fellow (an Indian spy we supposed) light out. Lt. Beck and I surveyed the surrounding country from the top of a hill, but could see nothing. Soon after Young first saw the man a couple of couriers from Eagle Springs came in reporting that 40 Indians had been seen across the Rio Grande at Ojo Caliente.[63] A party of five Indians on this side fired at some Pueblo Scouts and they returned fire – no one hurt. I wrote a communication to Capt. Gilmore this eve,' and sent it on stage. We'll take an early start & got in before noon a good deal. Chas. Palmer, the operator at Quitman, and I have gotten to be great friends – he is mighty nice. A coyote has just made an infernal yelp. Saw a jackass-rabbit this afternoon. Hope I'll get a letter or so in mail.

---

[62] Most likely George Young who served in the 10th Cavalry from 1878 to 1882 and is listed as a teamster. *Roster*, Fort Davis National Historic Site.
[63] Currently named Indian Hot Springs, Ojo Caliente is approximately thirty-five miles south of Sierra Blanca.

Eagle Springs, Texas

Aug 1st (Sunday)

Night before last and last night I had no chance to write as I had to copy for Lt. Beck – he thinks my name ought to be put down on the rolls as a temporary clerk.

When the West bound stage came by "Rocky Point"[64] Thursday eve' (our camp) the driver told us that Capt. Viele[65] and company were coming out as had been ordered by East bound stage the same eve. Between one and two in the morning a couple of couriers came in from Eagle with communication saying that a large party (60 or more) of Indians had camped that eve' on this side of the Rio Grande – they were sent on to Nolan.[66] They also reported that Capt. Viele would come.

---

[64] Rocky Point is what Robert called Tinaja de as Palmas, the name of the firefight Grierson used in his official report.

[65] Capt. Charles Delavan Viele served in the Regular Army during the Civil War, joining the 10th Cavalry in 1870 as Captain of Company C. He participated in the pursuit of Geronimo in Arizona, commanded the 1st Cavalry in the Spanish-American War, and was promoted to Brigadier General in 1904. Thrapp. Vol. 3.p. 1485.

[66] Grierson was camped fifteen miles west of Eagle Springs at a waterhole named Tinaja de los Palmas when he learned that Victorio had crossed into Texas. This word came from Capt. Nolan at Fort Quitman, who immediately dispatched Lt. Henry Flipper to notify Grierson. At this point Grierson knew that Victorio was likely to seek water at his location. With Lt. Beck, Robert, and six troopers, two of whom were teamsters, Grierson determined to hold the water until help arrived. Sending word by the east and west bound stagecoaches passing in the night he rallied his troops. Leckie, p. 224. Of his ride to bring the news to his colonel, Flipper wrote, "I rode 98 miles in 22 hours mostly at night, through a country the Indians were expected to traverse in their efforts to get back to New Mexico. I had no bad effects from the hard ride till I reached the General's tent. When I attempted to dismount, I found I was stiff and sore and fell from my horse to the ground, waking the General." Theodore Harris (ed.), *Black Frontiersman: The Memoirs of Henry O. Flipper* (Fort Worth: TCU Press, 1997), p. 34. A "tinaja" is a catchment basin or waterhole, and "palmas" is Spanish for palm. There are no palms in the area, so this probably refers to the large yucca, the true

Immediately on hearing this Indian news we went to work – put the transportation (wagon, ambulance and six Mule team) in positions at the side of the ridge, and then made two fortifications on top of the ridge by piling up stones – the rocks made a natural breastwork on one side. Our force consisted of 10; including teamsters, Papa, Lt. Beck and me. We made two first rate little forts & called them respectively – "Beck" and "Grierson." The rocks were very rough and we got our hands scratched like everything. We had our water and provisions put into our forts. Lt. Finley came up at 4 A.M. Friday saying that he had been ordered to escort Papa & party in to Eagle Springs. He had 15 men. Papa thought best to "hold the fort" & couriers were sent to Eagle for Capt. Viele. Lieut. Finley's men made a very strong fortification on the lower knoll of the ridge. After fortifications were made I lay down in one & slept till about 7:30 & soon after we ate breakfast. Just after we finished the vedettes halloed: "Here come the Indians!!!" We made for our posts immediately. The Indians came through a canyon in the hills S.E. of camp & got within a half mile before we saw them. Their intention was to cross northward. After considering for awhile Papa had Lt. Finley and ten men charge after a part of them who'd crossed the road – couldn't tell how many Indians there were at first – they kept coming through the hills. Several Indians hid in a hollow till Lt. Finley passed & then fired on his party – he had them on all sides of him & poured it into them thick & vice versa. The rifles sounded splendidly and you could hear the balls singing. Just as Lt. Finley was about to dislodge the Indians from behind a ledge, Capt.

Spanish dagger (*Yucca faxoniana*), which does grow around Quitman Canyon. Dr. Michael Powell, E-mail, April 6, 2017.

Viele's & Lt. Colladay's companies came in & in the smoke and dust took F. for Indians & fired on him – Finley thought they were troops at first but when they fired he thought they were Indians and returned the fire. He concluded if all those were Indians he'd better get back to our fortifications & ordered his men mounted and charged back to camp & lots of Indians following howling like coyotes. Lt. Finley's party killed two Indians & one of his men had his horse killed and the same man had his finger grazed by a ball. All got back the same time except the dismounted man – he got along as best he could – the Indians were nearly on him – he turned and fired his revolver & this checked them some. We then let fly from our fortifications at the Indians about 300 yds off & golly!! You ought to've seen 'em turn tail & strike for the hills. If this one man had only got back with the rest we could have waited till the Indians got very close to us before firing and have played hob with them (they supposed that Lt. Finley's party was the whole force). As it was the sons of guns nearly jumped out of their skins getting away.

When the companies came upon the Indians, Cap. Viele and Lt. Colladay were riding about 300 yds ahead of their troops. As Lt. Colladay[67] was dismounting an Indian shot him in the leg and broke his horse's leg. The Indian then shot at Capt. Viele as he was getting off. Capt. Viele then got good aim and killed the Indian dead. The companies had a lively fight with the Indians and five or more of them were killed and Davis of Capt. Viele's Company had his horse shot, and after fighting bravely was killed. After the Indians were driven into the hills the

---

[67] Lt. Samuel Colladay never completely recovered from his wound and died January 14, 1884. Heitman, p. 317.

companies came to our camp, and watered and rested – the Indians again attempted to cross & the companies again drove them back. In the whole engagement our side lost 10 horses, a mule and 4 more horses wounded besides the soldier killed.[68] Capt. Viele arrived about 11 A.M. and Capt. Nolan at 12:30. On the approach of Capt, Nolan the Indians became uneasy, and soon fled in great haste for the Rio Grande. We sent out to Co. "A" when we saw it coming and they came the last 8 or 10 miles at a lope. From all accounts and evidence it was the effective force of Victorio's command (about 100 men) that we were engaged with. It is remarkable how quick the Indians jump from their ponies, lie flat on the ground and blaze away. The Indians were wonderfully surprised to see the troops come from both directions, and how they concluded that it was bad medicine. Lt. Colladay was brought into Eagle in our ambulance and all of us came in here (Colladay's, Viele's & Nolan's Companies). Lt. Finley did splendidly and it is a wonder that he came out so well. If the Companies had recognized him, the Indians would have been still worse beaten. Indians lost 7 men killed, a number wounded, and some stock wounded.

All the Indians in the country couldn't 've dislodged us from our positions. If I'd've had a horse I would've gone on the charge with Lt. Finley. I wanted to go with several men over on a ridge, but Papa thought it best not to separate our force. Lt. Beck made some long range shots.

We got in about 5 P.M. I wrote (copying) for Lt. Beck till nearly 11 P.M. We took supper at Capt. Gilmore's mess.

---

[68] Private Martin Davis, Company C. Glass, p. 95.

Yesterday (Sat.) forenoon I wrote for Lt. Beck. About noon Young and I ate a lunch, took our rifles, ammunition, and a canteen, and Papa's glass [telescope] and struck out for the hills back (S.) of camp. We went up on the rocky point $1^{1}/_{2}$ m. S. of camp, and followed the ridge around in shape of a "C" – the view was splendid. We saw a white object nearly as far as "Rocky Point," and saw Carpenter's and Hunt's companies coming through Bass Cañon – Companies got in about 4:30 P.M., and the white object was an ambulance for Quitman. We had lots of fun rolling rocks off the tops (cliffs) of the hills. Young pried an immense rock off – it was worth the climb to see it go bounding along 150 ft. at a jump – it went nearly ½ mile down into a cañon. Two rocks in succession hit the same Spanish dagger about 600 yds off – this is singular. We followed an old trail and were just descending the last hill as a blacktail deer jumped up – I banged away at it on the run – if I only had my shotgun I could have killed it certainly. Young made some close shots at it a long ways off. I wish we could've killed it, for we are tired of eating "hog."[69] This deer got over ground most remarkably. I sprained my ankle when running over the rocks trying to get a 2nd shot. I only got 1 shot. We got back at 5 P.M. and supper was relished. On the mail I got a letter from Mama, and one from Ella Richardson with a photo. All well. Went down to Operator's tent with Mr. Berger. Talked a little to Palmer. The officers of the Co's. from Ojo del Viejo are well.[70]

---

[69] Salt pork or bacon, also called sow belly. Don Rickey, *Forty Miles a Day on Beans and Hay* (Norman: University of Oklahoma Press, 1963), p. 116.
[70] The supply camp at Sierra Viejo Pass, where there is a major spring.

Sunday, August 1st 1880

Wrote all forenoon for Lt. Beck. By George! I'll have to draw pay soon. Lt. Beck thinks I ought to, and would recommend me as a clerk. Mr. Berger stayed with me in my tent last night – we didn't get to bed till late as the tent was full of officers. Lt. Colladay, with Dr. Duvall[71] and a suitable escort, left about 1 A.M. for Davis – from there to Stockton.

Scouts are kept out all the time and are coming in often with news. Victorio is on the other side of the river, and Col. Valle, Mexican Army, is moving towards him. I would have gone hunting again today if I had not had so much writing to do. Have talked French, German & Mexican with Berger. He heard me [give] a good lesson in DeForno's. Well 14 pages is about enough for one job.

The soldier was buried here yesterday. The eve' we got here the west bound stage was attacked and the driver and a man with him killed – a mule was killed and cut up into steaks – this shows the Indians are hard up – other mule taken – this occurred about 10 M. from here (not far from our fight). The men buried here yesterday afternoon.

Monday, Aug. 2nd, 1880

About 10:40 Mr. Berger, Young, and I went hunting. Young had the Winchester, Mr. Berger Papa's rifle, and I took my shotgun and plenty of buckshot cartridges. We walked 10 or 12 M. altogether – went in a kind of a triangle – Southeast then West and then North (to camp) about 4 miles South we found a stream of running water 150 yds long with

---

[71] L.S. Duval, Acting Assistant Surgeon at Fort Stockton. *Annual Report*, p. 115

several pools, and in one of them there were bulrushes, moss, etc. A young bussard [buzzard] with the downiest white feathers was sitting on a rock near a pool – it wouldn't fly. I killed a snake near the same place. We had a nice bath in the largest pool, & Young and I were clear under water. The water is in a deep cañon. The grass round about is splendid, and there is a good place for several Cos. to camp. I went up a couple of high hills East before getting to our creek. Got home at 4 P.M. We had an appetite and a half for dinner. After dinner I put on clean underclothes and feel as sweet as need be. We saw no game – but plenty of deer dung and trails. I think I found a bear's den. Capt. Carpenter & Papa said to show them the place, we are going over in the morning, and I guess Capt. C will camp there. Papa wrote to Lts. Smither & Davis, and to Mama today. I made Lt. Finley and Dr. Gregg[72] a visit after supper. Quite cool.

In camp about 10 m. S.E. of Van Horn on the road 35 m. from Eagle

Wednesday, Aug. 4th, 1880

Yesterday morning I went with Capt. Carpenter to "Camp Longview" and his & Lt. Jones[73] cos. camped there – liked the place exceedingly – you can see away out on the plain, and over the tops of some of the hills at the other camp. Papa thinks it is a fine place. A soldier came back with me, and then Papa went up on the horse I'd ridden. They'd no more than gotten camp well made than a patrol came in saying

---

[72] C.K. Gregg, Acting Assistant Surgeon at Fort Concho. *Annual Report,* p. 116.

[73] Lt. Thaddeus Winfield Jones, West Point, joined the 10th Cavalry in 1872 serving in the regiment until the Spanish-American War where he commanded the 10th U.S. Volunteer Infantry. Heitman, p. 582.

Victorio with 125 men, lots of horses, etc. was moving north to the East of Eagle Springs, and was then 15m. South of the road. One of the soldiers had been wounded in the foot.[74] All of the companies were gotten ready immediately and we left at 3:30 and arrived at water $2^1/_2$ miles this side of Van Horn at 10 P.M. The command consists of Carpenter's, Jones', Viele's, Nolan's, and Collady's Co. (in charge of Ayres), and Capt. Gilmore's. A few men were left at Eagle to look after property. We present a very martial aspect when on the march. Capt. Gilmore's wagons (supplies), our am', and wagon, and Dr. Kingsley's[75] ambulance are along – the Dr. had just got his tent up at Eagle when we had to turn around again. We made our beds in the tent spread out on the ground last night. I don't know when I slept more comfortably – the air was cool and I was a warm as a bug in a rug.

Thursday

Got up before sunrise and started early. Met the stage & got mail. Papa had a letter from Mama, and I one from Knollenberg.[76] Lt. Mills has been

---

[74] The day before, August 3, Corporal Asa Weaver, Company H, engaged Victorio's band as they once again crossed the Rio Grande into Texas. "Corporal A. Weaver, with Pvt. Brent of H Company, and a small detail from other companies, while on picket at Alamo Springs, discovered Victorio's band of Indians after they had crossed the Rio Grande and had an engagement and running fight for 15 miles." Glass, p. 23. During this fight Private Willie Tockes of C Company lost control of his horse, which ran directly towards the Apache and Tockes was killed. William Leckie, p. 226.

[75] Byron F. Kingsley, Acting Assistant Surgeon at Fort Davis. In the *Annual Report*, p. 115.

[76] This is most likely a schoolmate of Robert's. The Knollenbergs were a large family in Jacksonville involved in the sale of tobacco and the manufacturing of cigars. Hillary Peppers, Adult Services Librarian, Jacksonville Public Library, Email, April 13, 2017.

sick with ague – he started for Davis on the stage from here today. The Cavalry are down in the flat, and Capt. G., Lt. Dodge & we are camped behind a little hill, from the flat top of which the flat can be viewed for miles and miles. Mr. Berger is along with us, and I talk "foreign" to him all I can – we had a long Spanish lesson today – have gone through nearly 8 lessons in DeForno's. We went a little beyond here today & stopped for a couple of hours, while McCarthy cut in. No important news. Victorio has not crossed the road up to nearly noon today. Hope we will be as lucky as before – if we can only meet him it will be hunky. A patrol has been sent to Rio Grande. Have just heard a man say that 75 Indians crossed 4 m. West of Van Horn about 3 P.M. today. Few minutes ago I knocked a big scorpion off my sleeve. Be in bed before 8:30. Pull out very early. Hope we have good luck.[77]

In camp at Rattlesnake Springs

Friday, Aug. 6, '80

I had just lain down Wednesday eve' when papa called me to arrange things for his saddlebags – intended to start immediately & with just pack mules, then thought it'd be better to take the wagon & ambulances as far as possible. Our outfit was ready to start at 11[p.m.].

---

[77] Upon learning that Victorio had crossed the Rio Grande and was headed north, Grierson determined to out march the Apache to the water at Rattlesnake Springs. "Grierson knew how to march, he had proved that in his raid of 1863, and he proved it again on a torrid August 5, 1889. He was on the moved at three in the morning to Rattlesnake Springs some sixty-five miles northwest, keeping a range of mountains between his command and the Indians. He covered the distance in twenty-one hours, arrived ahead of Victorio, and had ample time to prepare an ambush. Few, if any, commanders and their troops could boast of having outmarched a band of Apaches." Leckie, p. 226.

We sent word to the Cos. (camped near water in bottom), but about $1^1/_2$ hours after sending the man came back saying he couldn't find camp. You ought to've heard the swearing (I have been writing by camp fire light, and was stopped just now by alarm that Indians were coming into camp – I'm afraid I spoiled my boots putting out the fire. It was Carpenter's Co, coming in after being after Indians. I'll finish tomorrow – it's too hard writing in this fashion.)

Aug. 7[th][78]

This delayed us that time. We started at three o'clock Thursday morning – all five co's and the two ambulances & our wagon. Capt. Gilmore left early the same morning, and waited some distance out for Grevenstine's[79] train, and had it cut off from the road and come along with him. The Cav. Got here at midnight, and we (the ams & wagon) got here at 3:30. Altogether the Cav. Stopped about 3 hours – two hours for dinner and one hour in the morning for water – about 5 o'clock Thursday morning we crossed a high rocky ridge – it was a "tug" but the teams made it. About 15 miles from here was the last we saw of the Cav. (about sundown – or after – our mules were very tired, and all of us had to walk from there,

---

[78] Robert's description of the sixty-five mile march to Rattlesnake Springs.
[79] The teamster in charge of the supply train that Captain Gilmore was escorting during the campaign. Any major campaign required mule drawn wagons to transport the massive amount of materials, rations and forage required to keep troops in the field. Usually manned by civilian contractors, a train would consist of thirty or more wagons. For the Victorio Campaign Grierson had two supply trains. An excellent description of troops on campaign is provided in Douglas McChristian, *Regular Army-O: Soldiering on the Western Frontier, 1865-1891* (Norman: University of Oklahoma Press, 2017), pp. 450-492.

except for a couple of sick men in Dr's Ambulance). Now and then we got into the ambulance or wagon for a minute or so to rest our legs. We had no trouble following the trail, but our mules gave out, and Johnson (the ambulance driver) had to put his mules to the wagon, and took the two best mules of the wagon. We got along alright then with six mules to our wagon and the two to the ambulance. An Indian boy caught up to us, and this scared some of the men. I was the advance guard most of the time. I confess these daggers with their fan tops like an Indian feather head-dress have a terrifying aspect at night – here and there you'd step into a hole and jar yourself. My back was the only part that got tired, but I and all were very sleepy. The Cav. marched sixty-five miles in less than 18 hours. Papa and Lt. Beck were nearly frozen when we got here – neither had their overcoats. I would've been mighty uncomfortable if I hadn't've had Papa's coat, but of course I wish he had had it. It is astonishing what a great difference there is in the temperature of day and night here. Decidedly hot in the day and shivering cold at night. Lt. Beck and I got the Dr. to give us a little whiskey and we needed it. Papa curled up in the ambulance, and I made a bed on the ground, and got a couple of hours sleep before breakfast. You bet we ate – the first grub we'd had since noon the day before. I slept some more during the forenoon. It is a good position here behind a ridge, from which the plain can be looked over for a good ways. A courier came in yesterday morning saying the Indians were at the Fresno – he got into their camp without them knowing it, and you bet he got out without them knowing it too. He had a message for Kennedy[80] from Guadalupe Mts., and was bound for Eagle. This was splendid news. We intended to head them off, and we did. Capt. Viele "C" Co., and Lt. Ayres with "G" Co. moved southward in the forenoon, and about 2 P.M. we heard volleys. It was Victorio's main outfit, and seeing that were but 2 cos. charged for the troops, but just at this time (3 P.M.) Capt. Carpenter "H" & Lt. Jones "B" reinforced Viele, & the Indians, greatly surprised, fled for the hills and mountains. Capt. Gilmore's outfit (train) rounded the point of the hills soon after; a party of Indians made for them, but were repulsed very warmly. No damage was done to Gilmore's command, but the Indians had one badly wounded man, but managed to carry him off on their ponies. The Cavalry returned after dark without losing anything, but it was reported that three Indians were shot. The troops also captured two ponies from an Indian spy. The spy'd've been more valuable. Papa, Dr. Kingsley, Lt. Beck and I went out and met Capt. Gilmore. After coming back the Dr. & I took a bath in the salt lake north of here beyond the spring. The water is as clear as crystal and is exceedingly salty – also impregnated with sulfur, and only about 4 or 5 inches deep with alkali bottom. Our bath refreshed us like a sea bath would.[81] Dr. says the water is good for a certain disease. Coming back

---

[80] Capt. William Boyle Kennedy, a native of Ireland and veteran of the Civil War, joined the 10th Cavalry when it was organized, retiring as major in the 4th Cavalry in 1897. He was in command of the Pine Springs sub post in the Guadalupe Mountains. Heitman, p. 592.

[81] Robert was not as personally engaged at Rattlesnake Springs as he was at Tinaja de las Palmas and did not consider the importance of this fight. It was here that Victorio met his greatest defeat at the hands of the U.S. Cavalry, a defeat from which he would not recover. At this point, as Victorio scattered, Grierson once again sent troops to guard the mountain passes and waterholes. Three days before Rattlesnake Springs, Captain Lebo and K Company had captured Victorio's supply camp in the Sierra Diablo, and on

from the bath I went to water my horse at the waterhole – when he pulled away from me, and got mired nearly to the altitude of his excretory orifice; he drank all he wanted and then jumped out the other side – it is luck he got out so easily. The mosquitoes are quite troublesome here – the first place I've seen then in Texas. Guadalupe Peak about 40 m. from here, looms up beautifully. About 6 we get into the shade of the mountains on the west. Sierra Diablo – from then till morning it's cool. Capt. Gilmore brought detachments of Cav. & extra horses, and the Grevenstine train with forage – much needed.

Saturday, Aug 7th, 1880

Captain Carpenter and three companies were sent toward Sulfur Spgs.[82] 22 m. West of North this afternoon about 1:30. Sulfur Spgs. & this place (Rattlesnake Spg.) are the only two permanent water places in this part of the country, and it will go hard with the Indians. Shouldn't be surprised if they retreated to the Rio Grande. Capt. Lebo got in soon after Carpenter left. He had been on scout, and captured the supply camp of the Indians in the mountains west of here, finding about 25 freshly killed cattle. There had been a detachment of Indians at the camp, but seeing the Co. first, fled with precipitation. It is thought that the Indians are moving toward Sulfur Spgs. & that Carpenter will get a whack tomorrow. Captain Nolan & Co. went southward down the valley today but saw nothing.

August 11, Captains Nolan and Carpenter cut the Apache trail west of Fresno Spring. After Carpenter's horses gave out Nolan pursued Victorio all the way to the Rio Grande. Leckie, pp. 22-227.

[82] Sulfur Springs is at the north end of the Sierra Diablo and just south of the Guadalupe Salt Flats along U.S. Highways 180/62.

Capt. Livermore[83] with a Co. of the 8th Cav. got in late this afternoon. (I believe he's been on a surveying expedition locating new places for posts South of Davis etc. After the 10th Cav. had already selected the places.) He came in first with a couple of his Indian scouts – it he'd done that yesterday the Indians'd've scalped him. Oh, I forgot that he's baldheaded!! (Co. got in before dark with Lt. Pullman.[84]) His wagon train will not be in till tomorrow night & and left El Muerto the same time that Grevenstine left 9m. in advance of him! (Livermore's) Yet he says he 'rushed through'!!! This is perfectly absurd. West Point tactics and engineering.[85] I bet he'd be like a peeled banana if he'd made such a march as we did. "Rushed through" – golly how we all laughed when he went away (to see where to camp). He says that loading from his wagon to his pack mules delayed him – this oughtn't to have delayed him more than 20 minutes Lt. Beck says. If some Indians would get after him once

---

[83] Capt. William Roscoe Livermore, West Point, was Chief Engineer for the Department of Texas. He was assigned by General Ord to conduct a survey of West Texas, which coincided with Grierson's campaign. Ord reported, "One special surveying party under Captain Livermore, Corps of Engineers, chief engineer officer of the department, is now out with the view of obtaining sufficient information of the region embraced in the districts of the Pecos and Bravo to secure proper locations for the military posts, for which an appropriation of $200,000 has been made by the act of Congress approved April 16, 1889." *Annual Report*, p. 112. With an escort of troops from the 8th Cavalry, a well-equipped supply train and a Gatling gun, Livermore also scaled the second highest peak in Texas, which he named for himself. Jacobson and Nored, p. 111 & 118. It is obvious that Robert did not care for Livermore or his purpose.

[84] Lt. John Wesley Pullman, 8th Cavalry, was in command of Livermore's supply train.

[85] Grierson a non-West Point graduate was aware, as were many of his colleagues, that he was not held in the same esteem and found promotion more difficult than graduates of the Military Academy. Robert was well aware of this situation.

he'd learn something. Five wagons moved out this eve' for El Muerto to bring Lebo's forage.

This forenoon & before Carpenter left, I copied ten closely written pages for Lt. Beck. Two copies of the report to Adjutant Gen. Dept. One copy sent to Palmer, Operator at Quitman. Palmer has been sick – he sent to Eagle to me for whiskey – I couldn't get it. Berger wrote today for clothes, and I put in a line saying that I could obtain no whiskey, but I could send some of our gypsum water which ______ ______ __________.[86]

I wrote a postal to Mama too.

I wish Papa had gone with the troops yesterday after the Indians – the movements could've been decidedly better made and a lot of the Indians ought to've been captured. Papa wished he'd gone, but he supposed the movements would be made according to his directions. Lt. Read was a little – well not as he ought to have been – to Papa this afternoon when all the officers were talking in out tent. It is true he has a good sized head, but <u>he</u> is the only person I know who thinks it is compactly filled with brains. He said Victorio could be sitting on his ___ with a field glass & his legs hanging over the cliff (of the hills west) looking at us etc. etc. I don't see how Papa kept as cool has he did – I got hot, and it was all I could do to keep from saying something.

This eve' some ducks were seen on the lake, & I'm going down in the morning. (Well I've said most [of what] I wanted to say, but not in systematic order.) Last night was our first night's rest for 4 nights – three nights previous nothing but "cat naps" of short duration.

---

[86] One has to use one's imagination.

Sunday, Aug. 8, 1880

I didn't fall asleep till late last night, but I slept well. It gets very cool towards morning. Lts. Shunk[87], Finley, Read, & the two Drs. (Gregg & Kingsley) & I had a good time in the Dr's ambulance this forenoon. Studied Spanish & recited to Mr. Berger today. I've gone through 10 lessons. Some Indian scouts were sent up to the mountains today but saw nothing of consequence. I went down to the lake before supper but I could see no ducks. I thought I saw a flock about a mile & a half up the lake, but the mosquitoes nearly "clawed me up," and I was glad to get away. There was a breeze when Dr. & I were down the other day, & this is the reason the mosquitoes didn't bother as much. This morning Young & I took Lt. Beck's two horses & the Dr's to water. The Dr's and one of Lt. Beck's have sore backs – we bathed them in the lake water, & it will heal 'em up. When I went in the other day I was all chapped from walking, and the water smarted like everything, but it cured it right up. The Ranger Co. arrived this eve.' Bailer [Baylor] is the Capt's name.[88]

Monday, Aug. 9th, 1880

(written Tuesday 10th)

I didn't feel like writing last night. Yesterday morning Papa sent Berger & a lot of the Pueblo Indian Scouts to scour the tops of the Sierra Diablo. Capt. Livermore, Lieuts Read & Dodge, & Captain Gilmore also went, & after all had gone Papa had his horse saddled and went over to

---

87 Lt. William Alexander Shunk, 8th Cavalry, was with Livermore's escort.
88 Captain George Wythe Baylor, Company C of the Texas Rangers, was assigned to assist Grierson, especially by watching the Rio Grande crossings east of El Paso.

the base of the hill & and climbed up to, & went miles over the top of the mountains alone. These mountains are an elevated table land comparatively level on top. They found the dead cattle (killed by the Indians – I was mistaken when I said Lebo killed 'em – his men killed but two, and the large number were killed for meat by the Indians.) & the camp etc. From here it looks as if you could walk right up the hill from here, but they say it is 3 or 4 m. to the base & that after twisting around it is nearly six miles to the top, & that the mountain is 1,500 feet high – the little (looking) bluff on top [is] 150 ft. or more high. The view is fine. I wanted to go but Papa thought <u>I'd</u> <u>better</u> stay here. There is no reason at all that I shouldn't go, but I don't care. I know I can stand as much climbing & walking as anybody in the command. When we went up to Guadalupe Peak[89] two years ago I climbed more than Papa – the other day (coming here) I walked from before sundown till 3:30 the next morning – about 15 miles over the most infernal ground imaginable, thorns, holes, cactus, sand & bunch grass.

I went down to the lake again but saw no ducks – it was windy & the mosquitoes didn't hurt much. Captains Viele, Lebo, Baylor & I had a good talk in the ambulance in the forenoon. (Papa had gone.) I showed Drs. Gregg & Kingsley my pictures (photos) – they think they are "tony lasses." Dr. K. fell in love with Miss Rich. I studied several Spanish lessons towards eve' – am through the 12th. Folks were pretty tired when they got back from their climb. One of the Indians [Pueblo Scouts] fell

---

[89] In May 1878 Robert had also gone on an inspection tour with his father that included Forts Stockton and Davis, north to the Guadalupe Mountains, and south to Presidio on the Rio Grande. This trip took Grierson through much of the country over which he would pursue Victorio. Leckie and Leckie, pp. 251-252.

and hurt his side. Lt. Finley returned yesterday from Apache Springs, 8 m West of North where he went with a detachment of Co. "C" the eve' before. He saw no Indians but brought in two ponies & a gov. horse which came to him. We sent out some canteens by the men which go to the point everyday, & Lt. Finley brought back some good sweet Apache [Springs] water. Strange that my bowels are all right – nearly everyone else is <u>loose</u>. I eat cheese to counteract the effects of the water.

> Wednesday, August 11th 1880
> Headquarters District of the Pecos, In the Field
> Camp at Sulfur Springs, Gypsum Bottom, Hellfire Flat,
> Between the Sierra Diablo and Devilhoof Mountains,
> Beggar Co., Texas

These names themselves are diabolical but they do not misrepresent the place. The water is better and more air stirring than at Rattlesnake Springs. We left there with Capt. Viele's Company yesterday about 9:30 & got here about 5 P.M. – 22 m. we came slowly. Lt. Beck and Papa got here an hour or more before the rest of us. It was a hot uncomfortable ride. Captain Livermore & Co., Captain Nolan, & the rangers left about when we did. They pass through the Fresno [and] will meet Carpenter & Jones who left here last night, east of the mountains. It will thus be ascertained whether the Indians are still in the Devil Mts. [Sierra Diablo], or have left & where they have gone. A courier brought dispatches from Kennedy early this morning saying they had killed an Indian, & that there was but one horse killed in their first rumpus, though several horses were wounded.[90] None of us slept well last night. Guadalupe Peak looks grand from here – 25 m. The prettiest sight I've seen in Texas was the mirror-like reflection of the Devilhoof Mts.[91] in the salt lake as we left camp yesterday morning. If a photo had been taken of it, it'd've been difficult to tell when you had it right side up.

The starlight nights are lovely now the moon begins to loom up. I've seen it three nights in succession now over my right shoulder without trying to & I certainly will have good luck. Though I think this is humbug still I prefer to see it over my right shoulder. A good many meteors may be seen last night.[92] I saw two very bright ones – the last one shot half way across the heavens & was an intense blue color – the tail was visible quite a while after the head had disappeared – went from N.E. to S.W. Papa has gone up N.W. a few miles to the sulfur pools. We may move camp up there today. I took my Winchester's plates off this morning & cleaned and oiled the working parts, & cleaned the gun inside and out. Papa got back – about 12m. – saw some cattle trails. I had a long Spanish lesson with Mr. Berger today. It has gotten windy. When Papa was up on the Devil Mts. the other day he saw what he supposed to be a number of wild Indians coming towards him – he secreted & fortified himself between some rocks near the edge of a cliff so they could attack him from but one side. On nearer approach it proved to be Berger & his scouts.

---

[90] On August 4, Kennedy, who was based at Pine Springs, intercepted a group of Apache from the Mescalero Reservation headed south to join Victorio and pursued them back north.

[91] The mountain range across a plain to the east and parallel to the Sierra Diablo, listed on contemporary maps as the Delaware Mountains.

[92] The Perseid Meteor Shower occurs annually between mid-July and mid-August, peaking during the latter period.

Papa jumped from the rocks with a gun in hand & said: "Hallo Berger!"
Berger was much "stunned" as he said, for he couldn't imagine how Papa
got there and what he was doing.

Thursday, August 12th, 1880

Berger and 4 Pueblos went to Quitman today with dispatches – the
Indians have gone towards Mexico between Eagle and Quitman, probably
near "Rocky Ridge."[93] The troops sent couriers to this effect. I sent
postals to Charlie, "Mac," & Uncle John – all headed as in yesterday's
entry. I also copied a communication for Lt. Beck. It rained some today &
we got a taste of rain water – golly! How good it was. I studies the 13, 14,
& 15 lessons in De Fornos. This eve' the Dr. Kingsley & I went a few
100 yds. W. of camp & got some cactus canes, the wood is tough & when
the pitch is dry they look like basket work. Had good griddle cakes for
supper. When Dr. & I were out saw a jackrabbit – wish he had a rifle &
shot it – would be an acceptable change from "sow belly." I copied a
couple of communications for Lt. Beck this eve' – have been sent by
courier. All the Cos. are going to Eagle but Gilmore who comes here, &
probably Capt. Kelley comes with him. Transportation is to be sent to
Bliss for supplies.

Saturday, Aug. 14th, 1880

I didn't go to bed till nearly 10 last night and slept splendidly –
didn't wake up once. It rained from 2 A. M. till 4 P.M. with scarcely any
intermission – not very hard though – got a taste of rainwater again. Has

---

[93] Tinaja de las Palmas, Quitman Canyon

been cool. I read 106 pages in "Le Tour du Monde en 80 Jours" – am at [page] 172. Shannon's[94] train will be in soon – 11 wagons – 12 altogether. Shannon was here a little while ago – no mail but official. We have a big lot of grub coming – we need it. A train, perhaps, will leave for Bliss tomorrow – and I may get to go along. Forage, rations, and supplies on Shannon's train. I studied Spanish today – read about 15 lessons in the key – I'd gone that far in the grammar. Papa & the Dr. read in "Harper's half hour series"[95] today, & Lt. Beck & some of the officers played whist. The time passes quickly. Suppose we'll soon return to Eagle. Hope there'll be mail for me. I'll go to Bliss if I get the chance.

Sunday, Aug. 15th, 1880

Slept fine last night. Read about 50 p. "Around the World in 80 Days." Papa and I each had a bath today – both of us feel refreshed. It's been a pleasant day. We had a variety for supper this eve.' A wagon leaves for Capt. Kennedy's this eve' (one which came over with Shannon). Clouds on the Guadalupe looked very pretty today. It is raining there now. Dr. & I had a good talk this eve,' in regards to health, etc.

---

[94] James Shannon was a civilian teamster in charge of the supply train. At age sixteen, he arrived at Fort Davis in 1867. As a civilian employee of the Quartermaster Department, he was employed to assist with the move of the 9th Cavalry when the post was reestablished. From 1888 on he served variously as teamster, wagonmaster, foragemaster, and blacksmith. Interpretative handout on civilian employees at Fort Davis. Fort Davis National Historic Site.
[95] Short articles and sketches in *Harper's Magazine,* one of the most popular general interest publications of the period.

(written) Tuesday, Aug. 17th, 1880

We left Sulfur Springs yesterday about noon with Shannon's train. Dodge and Crevenstine's train left for Bliss for supplies a short time before. Cos. "C" (Viele) & "G" (Finley) are left at camp to await orders. Dodge returned via Quitman unless he should obtain supplies from Buell[96] before reaching Bliss, in which case they return to Sulfur. We came out about 16 m. West to the "Prieta"[97] before leaving the road at 5 P.M., then came a little East of South in the direction of Eagle. A very little water was found this side of the Prieta in a flat, & some of the animals which were lucky enough to be in front got a little. We saw the rain before getting there – it rained and blew all around us. I finished Jules Verne – reading going along in the ambulance. Got into dry camp, 35 m. at 11 & got through supper 12:15 [P.M.]. I took nothing but some "Liebig's extract of beef,"[98] (tea) as my stomach & bowels were out of order. I had taken some pills the night before (cathartic – I was threatened with piles[99]) – which had the right effect, but during the day I was foolish enough to eat three ripe prairie bananas[100] – they made me very sick – had the most intense stomach ache (as usual) but I finally succeeded in

---

[96] Col George Pearson Buell, 15th Infantry, was guarding the border in New Mexico. A Brigadier General of Volunteers during the Civil War, he was recognized several times for gallant and meritorious service, especially as commander of the pontoon train of the Army of the Cumberland, which he organized.

[97] Prieta translates from the Spanish as "dark"or brownish in color. Here it likely refers to the barren country being traversed, and is an opportunity for Robert to use the Spanish he was learning.

[98] A paste like substance of meat concentrate used in lieu of fresh beef.

[99] A common name for hemorrhoids.

[100] Most likely the *Yucca baccata* that grows through far West Texas and has a softer fruit than most of the other dryer, woody species. None of these species is known to be edible. Powell, Email, April 6, 2017.

vomiting, & then felt much better though weak & dizzy – the tea was splendid and made me sleep bully. I had some more this morning and this afternoon have felt like a fighting cock. We left camp about 6:30 – train earlier - & we stopped and watered from the kegs about 10, then came to a "jump off" of 200 or more feet. Papa found a good road to come down, & before three o'clock we got down all hunky with the train right after us. A train couldn't go back this way though except by going around some distance (where I think I saw a good place). Papa & Lt. Beck found lots of water, from late rains, in cañons where we stopped – all the stock was watered, kegs, canteens & bellies filled, this rest and refreshment did lots of good to both men and animals. If we hadn't found water we'd've been in an unpleasant condition to say the least. Lt. Beck went off to the left of the "jump off" coming this way & saw a deer, but it jumped behind a ledge before he could shoot. We are all now in camp about 6 m. from the hills, & in a good position on the north side of a small hill from the top of which a good view of the surrounding flat may be obtained. The wagons are formed in a line on the West side of camp with the tongues inward. We came 15 <u>long miles</u> & got here in very good season (soon after 4). We've traveled very slow today till after getting into this flat where the ground is solid – before this the road was the most of the way heavy. It is about 20 m. to Eagle – the Mts. loom up fine. Though this is a "hell of a country" in the truest sense of the word yet there are some pretty sites – the mountains in the distance, the clouds, some of the Spanish daggers, mescal, etc.[101] I got a lot of good canes near camp this afternoon & Papa,

---

[101] Grierson was coming down the west side of the Sierra Diablo towards Eagle Springs.

the Dr., Lt. Beck, & I have "raised cane" – all tinkering with them. Some of the men have been decidedly too cheeky & negligent lately. I had to go five times from Papa's tent to "my house" (the ambulance) to have various neglected articles brought to the tent. I told Sergt. to "hist" them & I'll raise a little "cane" in earnest the next time – Papa ought to have one particular man look after his duds as Lt. Beck does. The fact is that each man thinks someone else will attend to the gun, canteen, boots, overcoat, ammunition, etc. etc. so that nothing goes right. I guess things'll be better attended to in the future. If I don't get some letters from some of the "fair ones" at Eagle tomorrow I'll perhaps have another attack of the stomach ache.

Eagle, Wednesday, Aug. 18, 1880.

The train left camp about 5:30 and we about 6:40. Lieut. Beck, Dr. Kingsley and I came horseback and got in about 10:30 and watered our horses at the spring – it was nearly dry (Carpenter watered there yesterday I was told). The whole outfit got here before 11 o'clock. A stage man at the spring getting water told us there was plenty of water up the ravine west of the spring. The stage boss here lied – told us he knew of no water except the spring. The ravine was explored and plenty of water found – a temporary (at least) spring – it ran in so fast that the animals were watered. The Dr. found a good spring further up and plenty of water – the first was about $1^1/_2$ [mile] from here. Saw Carpenter, Shunk & Ayres today. "E" Company & "A" are on the river a few miles from Quitman – the other Cos. are at the "creeks" where Young, Berger & I went. I think we came more than 15 miles yesterday – nearly 20 & over 15 today. Papa met us near the spring and watered his horse.

A brother of Brown[102] (who was nominated for vice-president & who'se been gov. of Missouri) & another Saint Louis man went through on the stage for N.M. this afternoon. Say the papers are puffing our business up (as well they may). Several wagons, etc. – emigrants are camped here tonight bound for the West. Victorio & band are in the Candileria mts. 60 miles from Quitman. McCarthy "cut in" as soon as he got here & lines work well. Mr. Berger and 4 scouts are ordered to find the location of the Indians, & it's probable that we'll make a raid into Mex. Perhaps we'll go to Quitman tomorrow. Palmer attends to his duty right up to the handle. There was lots of mail here for us for a while but it was sent back to Davis – it will be down on tomorrow's stage.

Papa, Dr., and I have been working on our canes today – they are very pretty & strong – quite a curiosity – nearly full moon and one of the most lovely nights I ever saw. If I was in Jacksonville! Deer and jackrabbit were seen today. I wish I had seen the deer and been in shotgun range of it. I carried my 'Fod'[103] today – wish I had an auxiliary rifle barrel. I did some copying for Lt. Beck this afternoon.

---

[102] Benjamin Gratz Brown was former governor of Missouri, U.S. Senator and was the vice presidential candidate with Horace Greely on the Liberal Republican ticket defeated by U.S. Grant in 1872. White, p. 528, pp. 532-536.
[103] Shotgun

Friday, Aug. 20.

Spent a good part of the day in the ambulance studying Spanish but was dumb somehow & couldn't keep anything in my head. A man at Carpenter's camp of "H" Co. was accidentally shot by another man with a revolver through the leg – not dangerously. He and Dr. McLoon (who was here with the Dr. Kennedy all afternoon) went into Davis last night on the stage. Dr. McLoon is "busted" (not financially that I know of but by piles.) He was sick when he left Sulfur and a 65 mile ride piled upon his piles was too much of a pile (& he had done piles of riding before.) The caravan of stages & wagons of emigrants pulled out last night for the West. The stage man Johnson (& family) who was at [Fort] Worth when I came to Texas before, are of the number of emigrants. The mail didn't come in on the stage as our telegram reached there too late, but it came in on Livermore's train & we got it about 9:45 P.M. All of us had retired. I was suddenly waked up & <u>six</u> <u>letters</u> were handed me by Kelley (one of our Infantrymen of [the] outfit). I read them in bed (in ambulance) by moonlight. To say I was <u>glad</u> but faintly expresses my delight. The letters are from Agnes Lusk, May Wolcott, Davenport, E. Miller, Keeney and Mama.[104] M. Wolcott was in Mich. – promised to send a photo as soon as

---

[104] In the summer of 1889 Agnes Lusk was eighteen years old. She would remain in Jacksonville as a teacher and school principal. May Walcott was seventeen, and married in 1886. She was from a prominent Jacksonville family and her father, an abolitionist and "conductor" on the Underground Railroad, ran against Abraham Lincoln in the 1846 congressional election. William Davenport was Robert's age and likely a former schoolmate. Emilie Miller, eighteen, married in 1894. Proficient in shorthand, she taught at Brown Business College in Jacksonville and became the first female court stenographer for the 10th Judicial district of Missouri. The only Keeney listed in Jacksonville in the period was Joseph, occupation cigar maker. Peppers, Email May 23, 2017.

she returned to Jacksonville. Dr. Glover & Mr. Trotter of J' [Jacksonville] dead. Mr. Kepler and mules at Concho drowned. Lot's of papers came & today (20th) we've all been reading them. Everybody pleased with Gen. Grierson's movements against the Indians. Papa had a nice letter from Lt. Smither and two from Mama. I did lot's of writing for Lt. Beck today – Smither says, "Tell Robert I recognize his writing in many papers & he must go on the rolls." Gen. Ord is coming out on a tour of inspection & Papa says he'll talk to him – "That I'm clerk & interpreter & shoot at Indians with the Winchester rifle, etc., & Gen. Ord'll put me down as Wagonmaster." Lt. Beck says that'll do. I suggested that I'd be Wagonmmaster on detached <u>service</u> & that I'd certainly not delay the trains as I'd keep away from them entirely. H, B, & K Cos. all went to Ojo Caliente today. We may go to Quitman tomorrow or wait till next day. The papers (San Antonio at least) mangle the news in reference to our fights with the Indians. I fixed up a cane this eve'. Dr. Tanner completed his 40 day fast Aug. 7. My letters from the north were three weeks or more old.

Saturday, Aug. 20th, '80

Finished my cane this morning and wrote an 8 page letter to Uncle John this afternoon. Had a wind and dust storm late this afternoon. Dust blew in perfect clouds and down in the flat it towered way up. The clouds were intensely black & the thunder rolled and the lightning flashed but there wasn't much rain here. Rec'd a letter from Knollenberg this afternoon. One of the Tunnell girls is married. Papa rec'd a telegram this afternoon from Nolan at Quitman saying that a courier from "G" Co.

brings him word that another man accidentally shot himself (H Co.) & wanted a doctor. Dr. Kingsley and the men of K & H Cos. who came from Viejo yesterday have gone. The men are very careless it seems to me. Papa recd. a letter from Mama – all well. Writing so much has kind of tired me. A light has just been seen West of North of here about 6 miles or more. The Infantry Sergeant & some Pueblos are going out to investigate it (6:15 P.M.).

Sunday, Aug. 22.

I guess the light that we saw yesterday eve' was a dagger struck by lightning. The Sergt. & I went up to Livermore's camp (where Carpenter was camped) today. Left before 11 and came back before 2. Captain Livermore has a station on top of Eagle Peak. He and some of the rest were up there when it rained yesterday. It blew all their tents down at camp, rained very hard & hail nearly as large as hen's eggs fell. The officers are very pleasant there. Captain Livermore treated me to claret & rum punch – golly! It was good & I've felt fine ever since. Captain wanted me to stay to dinner & he'd come down in an hour, but as Papa'd thought he'd leave for Ojo Caliente today and thought [it] best to come back. I lunched with Pullman & Shunk. Captain Livermore killed an eagle the other day (but missed the deer). He and Dr. Price[105] called this afternoon. The doctor (Kingsley) got back at 4 o'clock with his sick man whom he found left at camp this side of Ojo Caliente – not a dangerous wound – pistol through the leg. Another storm coming up. Read all my

---

[105] Acting Assistant Surgeon M.F. Price was stationed at Fort Stockton but may have been accompanying Livermore as the doctor on his survey expedition. *Annual Report,* p. 115.

letters over again this afternoon. We got up to Captain Gilmore's nearly every evening.

Tuesday, Aug. 24th

In camp about 20 miles from Quitman near the East base of the Quitman Mts. & West of Rocky Ridge, South of the road. Left Eagle Springs at 2 o'clock yesterday & went into camp about 10 m. south of here – down the flat – at 8 o'clock – found plenty of water in 'dry creek' before camping (couple of miles). We came by Rocky Ridge – the Indians have been there & knocked down the walls. Papa found a sort of wrap made of calico & red flannel – we stuck it way up on a dagger bush. Papa, Lt. Beck, & I mounted our horses there & went all over the hills where the Indians were last seen – an infernal place – very rough. We found 3 dead Cavalry horses & saw 2 near Rocky Ridge.

Wednesday, Aug. 25.

Got dark last night before I could finish. We left camp at 8:30 this morning & got here (Quitman) before $1^1/_2$ P.M. The Indians [Scouts] were started earlier but stopped at E. end of canyon till we started through – cowards like all Indians.[106] It rained very hard in the Quitman Mts. today and the contrast of the heavy storm on one mountain and sunshine of the next – the rain and cumulus clouds – was fine. The dim edge of the mountains through the rain was very pretty. The mountains in the dim blue distance across the river [Rio Grande] (when coming out of this [west] end of the cañon) all went to make up a beautiful picture. We

---

[106] This is the only disparaging or racist remark in Robert's journal.

didn't strike the rain till we got here, and it's rained all afternoon. We had to wade through the creeks running from the mountains though, and just before getting here the <u>ground</u> <u>was</u> <u>not</u> <u>ground</u> but a sheet of running water for the distance of half a mile wide.

Lieut. Dodge with Crevenstine's train & Lieut. Budd[107] & Co. arrived from El Paso today and are camped 5 or 6 miles up the river. Dodge and Berger were here this afternoon. Dodge had a fine time in El Paso – senoritas, wine, beer, fruit, and agreeable people. Berger & scouts went nearly to the Candileria Mountains 70 miles W. of here & trailed the Indians there, but as this is an isolated range where they could be starved out & surrounded, he is sure they left for the Sierra Gusman, South of West of El Paso. They can't get into New Mexico as Gen. Buell has 19 Cos. distributed along the line. I could write a great deal about what Berger saw, but it is about 9:30 & "life is short." He went through some infernally rough and dangerous places.

Now about Wednesday.

Lieut. Beck, Papa, the Doctor, two Pueblos and I left camp mounted right after breakfast yesterday and struck out for Ojo Caliente. We made a trail of our own, & the devil of a trail it was too – rough is no name for it – we went over places that I supposed were absolutely impassible for stock. We had to lead our horses half the time when crossing the low spur of the Quitman Mountains. There was danger of our horses rolling down on top of you. I slipped and slid and separated my legs to an alarming angle a number of times. We passed through a steep

---

[107] First Lieutenant Otho Williams Budd, 4th Cavalry.

cañon on the S.W. side of the hills – found plenty of good rain water and a fine spring – cottonwoods, "tuli,[108]" etc. We struck Lieut. Read's trail at 'our spring' – this was about 3 miles above Ojo Caliente, and I'd a great deal rather be camped there than many other places. We stopped about half an hour. Carpenter, Ayres, Jones, Lebo, and Read are well and were very glad to see us. We left at 1:10 P.M. and followed the regular trail (Victorio's) back through the mountains. It is a fine trail and though it is very rough compared to regular ground, yet it is <u>level</u> compared with the trail we made going over. In passing through a gorge there was "un olor muy fuerte" (in other words 'an oppressive stink!'). Papa who was ahead investigated the smell, and it proved to emanate from three dead bodies of Indians, partially covered with rocks (buried), and which had been partly eaten by wild animals. There was the body of something else – either a dog or a boy – but the whole business raised such a smell that it nearly knocked Papa down. All the rest of us came by without seeing 'em but we smelt 'em "make no mistake." I was quite a piece ($^{1}/_{4}$ mile behind) and had been out of sight of the rest for sometime and I was not interested in smells at that time. Wagons can follow the trail to within 6 or 7 miles of Ojo Caliente. At "the end of navigation" a couple of wagons from Eagle had left forage for the companies – several men guarding it [were] sound asleep, and it was with great difficulty that we woke them up. Such men deserve to be shot or at least severely punished. It'd've been a good joke if we'd led their horses away or all shot off our guns and scared 'em.

---

[108] "Tule" is a common name for cattail (*Typha dominguensis*) that grows throughout the region. There are also bulrushes (*Bolboschoenus*) that grow in alkaline soil along the river near the site of Fort Quitman. Dr. Michael Powell, Email April 7, 2017.

While we were away camp was moved as ordered (but they went a little further than directed). Got to camp about 5:30 and demolished supper "con muchisimo gusto."[109] We picked up a horse that the Dr.'d left a couple of days before – had recuperated.

W. Aug. 25

Johnson killed a jackrabbit before striking the road this morning. I mention this because it's the first game that's been killed on the trip. Rec'd Mama's letter of 16th and Christie Higler's of 10th on arrival.[110] Mama enclosed a letter from Aunt Louisa. Williams of Band drowned 15th. Water has been very high there (Concho), Christie's letter is fine and the photo perfect (though she like all girls say it is "horrid"). Papa telegraphed to Mama this 'eve. Line all right all the way through. Stay in Dr. Kingsley's tent tonight – tired of ambulance since I got wet Monday night at Eagle – rained very hard. After 10 P.M.

Thursday, Aug. 26th, '80

Christie's letter was too much for me – it made me think of J'ville times & I believe I thought of everything I ever did, saw or expected to experience, so that I lay awake till nearly two o'clock: I looked at my watch for I thought I'd been awake a long time & it was 1:15 A.M. (today) & I didn't fall to sleep for quite awhile after. What time I did sleep though was sound. The Doctor grunted and seemed to be undergoing great agony & seemed restless. I thought that my flopping and turning kept him awake, but he says he slept splendidly. At one time he

---

[109] With great delight.

[110] Christie Higler's age is unknown. She was the daughter of German immigrants living in Jacksonville. Peppers, Email May 23, 2017

was about half awake & said: "What did you say Bob!" I told him that I was not aware of saying anything, & then he said: "Why didn't you? I thought you were talking right along."

It rained most of the night and over half of the day. I did a lot of copying (10 pages of letter paper) for Lieut. Beck. Papa sent his "summing up report" & it is very good. After Papa sent his report Mr. Marr sent an article concerning the movement of our troops to the Globe-Democrat – very good.[111] Beck & Dr. had baths in the river today & I will take one tomorrow. Lt. Nordstrom[112] came this afternoon – just in time for dinner – the front axle of his spring wagon snapped right in the middle about 100 yds below the telegraph office. He stays with us this eve'. Lucky that his buggy waited till he got here before "busting." He was somewhat daubed but not hurt. He landed unexpectedly & rather abruptly – somewhat prematurely. After supper I took a gun & went a on a little hunt up the river. I shot three times at "shit-pokes"[113] at long range but my shot was too small. I shot once at a dove. Sportsman's luck – tired, played out & sore – but a perfectly clean score. There is the most infernal

---

[111] The paper to which Robert referred is probably the St. Louis *Globe-Democrat*, which did cover the news from the West. Further on in the journal Robert identifies Mr. Marr as the brother of Mrs. General Gregg. John Irvin Gregg, a decorated major general of volunteers during the Civil War, was Colonel of the 8th Cavalry stationed in Arizona. He retired in 1879 due to injuries received in the line of duty. This is most likely the Gregg referred to. Thrapp, *Encyclopedia*, vol. 2, p. 586. At another point in the journal Robert explains that Mr. Marr was from the El Paso area and had a large farming operation there. Marr seems to have no official capacity and just came down the river out of curiosity to see what was happening.

[112] First Lieutenant Charles Eben Nordstrom rose from the ranks during the Civil War and joined the 10th Cavalry when it was organized. He was in charge of the Pueblo Scouts. Heitman, p. 750.

[113] A heron. Kelly Bryan, Texas Naturalist, personal interview August 26, 2017.

jungle of briers, willow, grass, mud, trees, sloughs, 'ad infinitum.' I found my way back by the Mountains & the direction of the river. I think I walked over 6 miles. I got damned badly mixed in a slough site, but I slew no game by a damn sight. It was too dark to shoot when I finally got around the slough to the old post where I saw & heard lots of doves and killdeers.

Four shots I'd fired & made a clean score. Had been lost and mired & you bet I swore. And as I was tired as I ever'd been before I rested my weary stern on a cottonwood log. And as I listened to the killdeers chirping along the bog,

> And gazed at the dark clouds above.
> I thought I missed my dove,
> And I doubted if it was a very good joke,
> To waste three loads at the wary shitpoke.

We have been telling hunting and Indian stories this eve'. This is the Mr. Marr whom we met in the Guadalupe's in '78. He is mighty nice & the brother of Mrs. Gen. Gregg.

Friday, Aug. 27, '80

Slept fine last night & Papa & I took a refreshing bath in the river before breakfast & put on clean duds. Johnson washed clothes for us today. The Doctor put on lots of dog with his boiled (biled) shirt, linen coat, [and] 'scotch breeches.' Lieut. Beck looked in a condition to mash anybody (if he sat down on 'em), Dr. Finley is a fine fellow; he called on us – also Capt. Kelley & then our outfit went up five miles in our ambulance to the camp. Saw Hunt, Flipper, Finley, Nolan, Nordstrom, Kelley & Dodge went up with us. Dodge sometime before. Dodge is

A.C.S. & A.Q.M. in the field.[114] Papa got some commissary stores – at my request he was so kind as to get some sardines – that's the kind of sardine he is. Papa sent to El Paso for a lot of wine & Dodge got him a 10 gal. keg. A box of fruit was sent on to Mama. Dodge has a keg of wine. We poured the wine from a water keg into a horse bucket & dipped out with cups like you would water, but I tell you that I hadn't <u>oughter</u>.

I.

I felt as careless as a gypsy,
Being just a little tipsy,
And you ought to've heard me laugh;
I was as jolly as a regimental,
And I didn't care a Continental,
But I drank but a cup & a half.

II.

"I'm willing to stake a 'quartah,'
That I can drink it like 'Watah'!"
Said the A.D.C: "So give us a taste,"
You ought to've seen him <u>grin</u>,
As he put pint upon pint <u>in</u>,
But he suddenly had no time <u>to waste</u>.

III.

"I has no bottom," said the 'Doctah,'
And you'd been shocked 'sah,'
To see the way he drank it down;
But it struck bottom, "make no mistake,"
For it gave him an awful stomach ache,
And he was as mad as a mangy 'houn.'

---

114 Assistant Commissary of Subsistence and Acting Quarter Master.

Altogether we had a fine time. Mr. Marr has given me a very kind invitation to go with him to El Paso. He has a fine fruit place – 15 acres – the only place this side of the river of the kind. He has to leave Mrs. Marr alone a good deal, & says he'd like to have a male about the place in his absence. There is a thin shade of a possibility that I'll go – perhaps too thin.

Lieut. Beck & Dr. Finley.[115] Have been across the river this eve on a "tear' – two old women and one virgin on to [about] 14 are there. The subject demands an immediate investigation – i.e. the one 'virgin' on to 14. I have my shot gun loaded with buck shot & if the coyotes keep up such an infernal serenade as they have for the last few nights, I'll endeavor to administer a quadruplex concentrated dose of cathartic plumbum plum pills.[116]

Sat. Aug. 28

I shot 4 killdeers before breakfast – got but three of them. Did some copying for Lt. Beck & wrote a boss letter 6 pages long to Mama. Ate some grapes today that they brought from over the river last night. This eve' we ate some watermelon (sandia) that the Dr. Finley bought from a Mexican – not very good. It has sprinkled some this evening. Lieut. Nordstrom took dinner with us & he says that's what he came for. I cleaned my gun & am ready for the coyotes again – they didn't sing last night. I shaved this morning – have left on my moustache & side

---

[115] Acting Assistant Surgeon Samuel Moore Finley is listed as assigned to Camp Pena Colorado, a sub post of Fort Davis near present Marathon, Texas. In the *Annual Report,* p. 115.
[116] Lead shot.

whiskers. "I don't look as much like a hedge hog as I did." I feel better too.

Aug. 30 '80

In Camp (en route from Quitman to El Paso) about 35 m. from Quitman between Camp Rice[117] & Hawkins.

We left Quitman at 11:10 A.M. Stopped a while at "Camp [Rice]:" left there at 1 and got here at 8. This is a queer country – plenty of water in the river but no grass in the bottoms – go out on the plains & there's grass but no water. As far as grass is concerned it is a perfect desert along the river, though the numerous cottonwood trees & green looking tornia,[118] etc., have a refreshing appearance to the eye. The soil looks good & there is a luxuriant growth of weeds, but not enough grass between here & "Camp" to feed a jackrabbit. The Doctor left his heavy ambulance at "Camp" & took Dr. Finley's lighter one. It is the most devilish thing to ride in ever I saw – worst than a "<u>jerker</u>."[119] You never know in what position or part of the concern you'll be in the next moment. I rode part way in it. The road has been sandy a good deal of the time. We watered at a lagoon 3 or 4 m. below here & I'd've camped there but the mosquitoes were too familiar on short acquaintance.

---

[117] Camp Rice was a sub post of Fort Davis and not a formal military post until 1881. In 1882 it was moved closer to the Southern Pacific Railroad, its present location. In 1886 it was renamed Fort Hancock in honor of General Winfield Scott Hancock. Frazer p. 151.

[118] Tornillo, the common name for the Screw Bean Mesquite, *Prosopis pubescens*

[119] A light, short, and narrow two-seat open passenger wagon. Nick Eggenhoffer, *Wagons, Mules and Men: How the Frontier Moved West*, (New York: Hastings House, 1961), p. 162.

Dodge's train left for El Paso yesterday – we'll overtake it tomorrow. Berger is with us. The Doctor was the very picture of discontent today – rough, dusty, etc.

Yesterday. I copied a good deal for Lt. Beck. Line was down and Palmer & Robinson (Soldier of "F" Co. 10th) left in the afternoon to go as far as the cañon to fix it if found down there. The operator was tight before he left, and Robinson took a <u>nip</u> too – they had a bottle of aguardiente[120] along & both must've been very drunk. About dark when the stage passed them in the cañon Palmer charged down at it from a ridge yelling like an Indian, & the stage mules became frightened, the driver supposed it to be Indians, fired at him (but didn't hit him – as the stage which came in this morning reports seeing him [Palmer] 6 miles this side of Eagle at 11 last night.) Orders were to not go further than in [the] cañon. Robinson probably was so drunk he didn't know the way back, wandered around all night, lost his carbine, wore out one of Papa's riding horses, & tore the shoes off it. Palmer has one of Papa's horses just sent from Concho, & Papa's equipments. The horses are all left at Nolan's camp in charge of Graham[121] of "D" Co. who's been 'lanced.' Robinson is left here to groom horses and straighten up. He'll have to pay for his gun. Palmer sent word by stage which got in this morning that he'd be down tonight on [the] stage. He's acted too damn smart lately, and Papa is

---

[120] Often used as generic term for a distilled liquor. Usually potent.
[121] The only soldier named Graham who was an officer and served with the 10th Cavalry was George Wallace. He was cashiered August 1870 and reported to have died in 1875. Heitman, p.467. The Roster of soldiers who served at Fort Davis listed no Graham who served during this period. *Roster Data Base.* "Lanced" meant one was given a temporary field promotion. McChristian, *Regular Army-O, p.*

going to have him removed. He's wild about his wife – just married a short time before coming out. He's rather a "<u>rip</u>" & not such a nice sort of fellow as I thought.

We had some venison yesterday & this morning which Nordstrom gave us. He is "Commander in Chief" of scouts & and some of the scouts killed the game. Flipper says that Palmer drank 6 bottles of aguadiente in 4 days. It's strong as lye – I'm not lying.

Dr. & I took a bath in Rio Grande this morning before breakfast, I, of course, waded over to Mexico. The river has fallen a great deal since we were there before.

Thursday, Aug. 31st. 1880

(Written the first chance I got at Fort Bliss, Tex. Friday, Sept. 3rd. '80)

Left camp about 9 A.M.; arrived at San Elizario[122] about 1 P.M.; stayed there visiting Mr. Miller & Mrs. Ellis till after 3 & arrived at Ysleta[123] about 5 P.M. where we camped on the Plaza with Dodge's train. It is about 18 miles from where we camped to Hawkins, and 7 miles from there to San Elizario & from the last place to Ysleta 15 miles – 40 march. I walked ahead from Camp about a mile hunting. I killed a hawk on the wing – dead – took the tail feathers & put in my hat, but concluded I looked too much like an "Injun," & took them out when I got to San Elizario. I had shot at a coyote but missed it. I shot a crow on the wing out

---

[122] San Elizario, located fifteen miles downriver from El Paso was, except for brief periods in 1854 and 1866, the county seat of El Paso County. As an agricultural area San Elizario was known for its produce, especially fruit and grapes. *The Handbook of Texas*, vol. 5, p. 838.

[123] Yslata, now absorbed by the greater El Paso metropolitan region, was another fertile agricultural area along the Rio Grande. Ibid. vol. 6. p. 1134.

of the ambulance, a chaparral cock on the run when the ambulance was going. I missed more shots than I hit, however. The road keeps right along the river valley all the way from Quitman to El Paso – some places very near to it. The "sake"[124] extends about six miles below San Elizario & from this point to El Paso there are ranches along the river & the soil is very rich, and altogether it is "an oasis" between the deserts of Texas & Northern Mexico.

At San Elizario we stopped & saw a sick American – Mr. Miller who was in the Union Army during the war. He has a nice looking young Mexican wife. He looks a great deal like Lincoln – "each particular hair stands on end like quills upon a fretful porcupine." He has quite a nice place – farm. We bought a nice watermelon & we ate a fine one there. Dr. Kingsley gave him some medicine & he gave the Doctor a muskmelon. We then saw "Nick" Kohlhaus who has charge of Mrs. Ellis' place. Mrs. Ellis is a "well off" Spanish widow & has a fine vineyard & fruit place. "Nick" is a lively German; he took us all over the place and we had all the pears, apples, peaches & grapes we could eat. The grapes are the El Paso variety which are peculiar to this vicinity. We were introduced to Mrs. Ellis & the house is one of the best adobes in this country – you might think yourself in New York, the house is fixed up so nicely. One large hall – dining & dancing hall is frescoed in Dutch – this rather spoils the look of it.

It is pretty much of a town all the way from San Elizario to Ysleta – ranchos all along. At Ysleta we stopped at Lowenstein's – a German Jew's –

---

[124] Acequia, the primary channel for a water or irrigation system.

till our wagon caught up & then camped.[125] We were treated to beer, wine, aguadiente, cigars, there. He is a merchant. After fixing up a little, Wiggins had our supper ready & then we called on the Schutz brothers, merchants & Ger. Jew like Lowenstein.[126] Didn't get to bed until after 11. There is a Catholic church at Ysleta several hundred years old, & other very old buildings. Buildings if properly made of adobe last a great while. The usual size of adobe [blocks] is 11 X 22 X $4^{1}/_{2}$ – though they are made of various sizes – the ones for some fences being 3 or 4 feet long (sometimes larger) $1^{1}/_{2}$ or more wide & about a foot thick. The pear trees grow as large as a good sized live oak of Texas, & I wouldn't believe they were pear trees till I saw the fruit on them. The grapes are large & deliciously sweet, & the pears, peaches & apples grow to a very large size.

Wednesday, Sept. 1 '80

Left camp about 9:30 After breakfast I went over to Schutz's & looked around the mill – they have a pipe sunk into the ground & get fine water. I gave both the Mr. Schutz canes of "balicoyote."[127] I had a good time talking German with them & Mr. Lowenstein; he came up with us in

---

[125] Moritz Lowenstein was a merchant who arrived in the El Paso area at the time of the Civil War. He married a local woman and was the Ysleta Postmaster through the 1870s. He eventually owned numerous properties, including a hotel in downtown El Paso. Born in 1836 he lived until 1929. Bernie Sargent, El Paso Historian, Email received August 1, 2017.

[126] Max (Moritz) and Sol (Solomon) Schutz were Ysleta merchants who arrived in 1871. Max was the Postmaster in the 1880s and instrumental in bringing an electric rail line to Ysleta from El Paso. Sol was the third mayor of El Paso from 1881 to 1882. Sargent Email.

[127] The giant reed *Arundo donax*. Dr. Michael Powell, Email received May 25, 2017.

our ambulance. Before leaving town we stopped at Mr. (Col.) Baylor's.
He plays the violin well & he has a very pretty daughter about 15 or 16
years old who plays the piano & sings well. Mr. B. plays too. We were
perhaps half an hour – perhaps more - & all of us enjoyed it. We
would've driven past but I thought it must be the place from hearing the
singing. We got here (El Paso) between 12 & 1 but didn't stop longer than
to get Lt. Kinzie[128] & go up the river a mile to the new post, & in the
meantime camp was located near Dodge's train on the open space N.W.
of & near the post.

"Continued in a book hooked from the field desk."

---

[128] Lt. George Herbert Kinzie, 15th Infantry, served as an enlisted man
during the Civil War,and was stationed at Fort Bliss. Heitman, p. 602.

Appendix One: Colonel Grierson's *Report* to the Secretary of War

Headquarters District of the Pecos,

Fort Concho, Tex., September 20, 1880

Sir: I have the honor to report that in the latter part of May, soon after my return from the expedition to the Mescalero Agency, New Mexico, Generals Hatch and Pope reported that Victorio's band, largely re-enforced by Mescaleros and other Indians, was moving toward the Mescalero Agency, and thus caused troops to be again ordered into New Mexico from this district.

Between May 21 and June 23 numerous telegrams were received, giving rather indefinite or complicated instructions for my guidance, occasioned, no doubt, by the difficulty in determining the question as to whose command the troops of this department would be under after entering the Department of the Missouri.

From what I knew of the hostile Indians and their whereabouts, I felt confident that they would not go to the agency, as indicated, and telegraphed you June 4 to that effect. Soon after Colonel Hatch reported that they had crossed into Mexico, south of Fort Cummings. As my orders still required me to proceed to New Mexico, and believing that it would be a great mistake, under the circumstances, to move the troops northward out of my district, and thus leave the country unguarded, I telegraphed you June 24 that it would be more judicious to increase the force in the western part of the district of the Pecos, toward the Rio Grande and Guadalupe Mountains, and thus have troops in position to be promptly concentrated to intercept and punish the marauders in case they attempted to cross into Texas, than to wear out the troops in scouting northward into New Mexico at that time with a hope that the Indians would come to the troops to surrender.

On the 28th of June I was informed, by telegraph from department headquarters, that my views, contained in telegram of June 24, had been approved by the Lieutenant-General, and that I could make my arrangements and dispose my troops accordingly.

Therefore, I at once moved Companies A, G, and I, Tenth Cavalry, from Concho, west, and made such further disposition of troops available for the field as would be best to meet the emergency. I arranged with Lieutenant Tingle, superintendent Texas division military telegraph to take an operator with me and have another sent to Fort Quitman: and leaving First Lieut. Robert G. Smither, adjutant Tenth Cavalry, Acting Assistant Adjutant-General, in charge of records and office – detailing First Lieut. William H. Beck, Tenth Cavalry, then at Fort Davis, as A.D.C. and A.A.A.G. in the field – I left Fort Concho July 10 to join the troops already *en route* to the West.

Under the date of July 13, Colonel Valle, Mexican army, reported from Carrizal, Mexico, that his command, consisting of four hundred and twenty men, would take the field on the 14th against Victorio and his band of hostile Indians, and that a force of one hundred and twenty cavalry was at that time following the trail towards Eagle Springs, Tex. This information I received at Fort Davis on the 18th, and at once ordered Lieutenant Mills, Twenty-fourth Infantry, then at Eagle Springs, in command of Pueblos, to throw his scouts out along the Rio Grande to closely watch and report the approach of the Indians; and I took the necessary measures to increase the force at Viejo Pass, Eagle Springs, Quitman, and the Guadalupe's, giving such instructions to the officers in command as would insure concert of action, and prompt concentration of troops at any threatened point.

These arrangements completed, I left Fort Davis on the 20th, and arrived at Viejo Pass on the 21st. On the 22nd I received your telegram of that date, informing me of the construction of the district of the Bravo, mainly taken from the southern part of my district. I arrived at Eagle Springs on the 23rd of July, where I learned that the Indians were then in the vicinity of Ojo del Pino, Mexico, about fifty miles to the southwest, near which point an engagement occurred a few days before between the Mexican advanced force and Victorio band; the main force of the Mexican troops then being near Fort Quitman. I at once communicated by couriers with the officer in command of the Mexican forces, who had been previously informed of the disposition of my troops. In answer, from the Barracho Mountains, Mexico, Colonel Valle confirmed the report of the engagement referred to, in which four Indians and three horses were killed, and the troops lost one man killed, three wounded and from ten to twenty horses driven off by the Indians.

On the 25th I received a telegram from department headquarters, informing me that the commanding general desired me to retain command of the region embraced in the district of the Bravo until the arrival of Colonel Shafter, then at San Antonio.

On the 27th I proceeded to Quitman; and on the 28th, to my surprise, the Mexican troops returned opposite that point entirely out of provisions, having exhausted whatever supplies they may have had and not captured by the Indians.

On account of their destitute condition, having had no food for three days, I furnished Colonel Valle, subject to approval of higher authority, one thousand pounds of flour, and eleven hundred and thirty pounds of grain. This issue was promptly reported, and my action has since been approved by the honorable Secretary of War. Colonel Valle informed me that he was authorized to cross into the United States, and had orders to pursue the hostiles until destroyed or captured, and that so soon as he obtained additional supplies, expected daily, he would again move against the Indians.

As the Mexican troops were thus withdrawn from the front of the Indians, and believing that the latter would at once attempt to cross northward, I left Quitman, on the 29th, for Eagle Springs, determined to intercept them. While *en route*, and near the east end of Quitman Cañon, an Indian was observed on top of a ridge near the road, who, upon being fired at, quickly fled. Soon after, I was met by couriers from Captain Gilmore, commanding officer at Eagle Springs, bringing the information that the Indians had crossed the river, and that the patrols had been twice fired upon by them. Deeming it my duty, I camped directly in their line of march, and at the only water for a long distance north. I then had with me First Lieutenant William Beck, Tenth Cavalry, one non-commissioned officer, and five privates – two of whom were teamsters – and my son Robert K. Grierson, who, just through school, was out in search for adventure and suddenly found it.

I sent orders, by stage [coaches] passing during the night, for the cavalry at Eagle Springs and Quitman to proceed immediately to my camp at Tenaja de los Palmas. At 1 a.m., July 30th, couriers brought report that that the patrols had again been fired at, one scout killed; and that the main body of the Indians were encamped the evening before, south of me, only ten miles distant. Having a thorough knowledge of my position and surroundings, I strengthened my camp with such means as were available, and sent the couriers on to Quitman, to hasten forward Company A, Tenth Cavalry.

On account of the hazardous position I was thought to be in by the officers at Eagle Springs, instead of the cavalry coming, as ordered, a detachment of fifteen men of Company G, Tenth Cavalry, under Lieutenant Finley, reported at 4:00 o'clock a.m. for the purpose of escorting me to that point. As I had no thought of being escorted there, or anywhere else, I immediately sent two of these men back with peremptory orders that all available cavalry be at once sent to my support. Being well supplied with ammunition, water, and provisions, I was confident of my ability to hold the position until their arrival, or so long as necessary.

About 9 o'clock a.m., the Indians were observed approaching in force, but seeing our strong position, they flanked off to the east, endeavoring to cross the road at a safe distance. With a view of preventing them, and, and to make known their position to Captain Viele, then approaching from Eagle Springs, and believed to be near, I ordered Lieutenant Finley, with ten men of his detachment, to charge and engage the Indians – the object being to unite our whole force against the enemy.

Lieutenant Finley carried out his instructions handsomely, briskly engaged the Indians, and, although they were in more favorable positions and vastly superior in numbers, held them in check until the arrival of Captain Viele, about 10 a.m., when, unfortunately, the advance of the latter mistook Finley's party for Indians, and fired upon them, causing them to withdraw to our position, pursued by a large force of the enemy, who, when they approached sufficiently near, were again vigorously repulsed and driven back in great confusion. At the same time Captain Viele's command was having a hot fight with the Indians, who were endeavoring to prevent his further advance. Soon Captain Nolan was seen advancing with his company from the west. A portion of the Indians, observing this, withdrew southward, and Captain Viele, forcing his way though, drove the Indians from a ridge south of our camp and joined us soon after. The Indians then made another attempt to cross north, but were again driven back by the cavalry. Captain Nolan advanced rapidly for the last six or eight miles, and, upon his near approach, the Indians scattered and fled in great haste and confusion toward the Rio Grande, none having succeeded in going north.

We, undoubtedly, fought Victorio's whole effective force, and in entire engagement, which lasted four hours, seven Indians were killed and a large number wounded. In the fight Lieut. R.S. Colladay, Tenth Cavalry, was wounded, and Private Davis, Company C, Tenth Cavalry, killed. Ten horses were killed and three horses and two mules wounded.

Scouting parties were promptly sent to follow the trail and watch the movements of the Indians, whose camp was found near Bosque Bonito, Mexico, opposite Ojo del Alamo, and about thirty miles below

Ojo Caliente. This information was at once forwarded to Colonel Valle, who was marching down the river from Quitman. He, for some reason unknown to me, moved immediately in the opposite direction, and soon after passed Quitman *en route* to El Paso.

Being convinced that the Indians would next attempt to pass north near Bass's Cañon, I increased the force at Eagle Springs; ordered Company E, Tenth Cavalry, from Stockton; Company K, Eighth Cavalry, from Davis, west; Company K, Tenth Cavalry, to scout through the Carriso Mountains and Sierra Diablo, and advised the commanding officer at Guadalupe Mountains of the probable approach of Victorio's band.

On the morning of August 3rd, a detachment of cavalry and scouts had a fight near the Alamo with the Indians, who had crossed into Texas the day before; one soldier was wounded and one still missing. Several Indians and ponies were shot. The force was estimated at one hundred and fifty. I at once moved my entire force from Eagle Springs, and headed them off at Bass's Cañon, and finding that they had gone eastward between the Van Horn Mountains and the river, I marched that night, and camped near Van Horn's Mountains, and early next day moved my command in front of the only pass where they could go through west of Capote.

While guarding these passes, southeast of Van Horn's and scouting towards the Rio Grande, to prevent the Indians passing southward or eastward to the settlements, they slipped through west of Van Horn's the evening of August 4th. This information was received from my patrols a few hours after, and I at once got my command in readiness and moved northwest, keeping a range of mountains between my command and the Indians, which effectively prevented their observing the movement. I left camp, ten miles nearly south of Van Horn's station, at 3 o'clock a.m., the 5th, and reached Rattlesnake Springs at 11:45 p.m., making a march of sixty-five miles in less than twenty-one hours, without the loss of an animal, and found myself, as intended, in advance of the Indians.

During the night I ascertained the location of the enemy, and early on the morning of the 6th placed Companies C and G, Tenth Cavalry, Captain Viele commanding, in Rattlesnake Cañon to await their arrival. At 2 p.m. the Indians were seen moving towards the troops, who held their fire until it was judged they would approach no nearer, when the troops opened upon them by volley, creating great confusion, and causing them to scattered in every direction.

The Indians seeing the smallness of the force opposing them, moved out in strong numbers to attack, endeavoring to work their way to water. At this time, Companies H and B, under Captain Carpenter, made their appearance, and after a few well-directed volleys, caused the disconcerted Indians to flee and again scatter in the hills and ravines.

At 4 p.m., Crevenstine's train guarded by company H, Twenty-fourth Infantry, and detachments of cavalry, approached about eight miles southeast, rounding a point of the mountains. The Indians seeing this, immediately sent a party to attack. Again they were astonished at the warm reception they met. Captain Gilmore vigorously repulsed them, and compelled their rapid retreat, with a loss of one Indian killed and several wounded.

The bewildered Indians then hastily fled toward the Carriso Mountains, pursued by the troops under Captain Carpenter.

Soon after, parties of Indians were seen coming from a cañon between the troops and the camp, evidently with the intention of attacking the pack trains and getting to the water. They were, however, soon obliged to retire.

It is impossible to tell the entire loss of the Indians, owing to the broken character of the country. Four were known to have been killed, and it is certain that many were wounded. A few ponies were captured. I am happy to state that in this engagement the troops suffered no loss.

During the day information was received from Captain Kennedy that, on the 4th of August, a detachment of his company, while following a trail into a cañon north of Bowen Spring, Guadalupe Mountains, was suddenly attacked by Indians. The soldiers held their positions for two hours, losing one man killed and several horses shot; loss of Indians unknown. Subsequently, Captain Kennedy attacked and pursued these Indians towards the Sacramento Mountains. In the several skirmishes one Indian and one squaw were killed and a few ponies were captured.

On the 7th Captain Carpenter was sent with three companies to Sulphur Springs, near the Salt Plains, to hold the water, scout the country as far as practicable, and to prevent the Indians passing north; and Captain Nolan was sent southward into Rattlesnake Cañon to scout towards the Carriso mountains.

Captain Lebo, with Company K, Tenth Cavalry, arrived at 2 p.m., having carried out his instruction is a highly satisfactory manner. He thoroughly scouted through the mountains to Sulphur Springs, and struck a trail and followed it to the tops of the Sierra Diablo, where, on August 3rd, he captured Victorio's supply camp, which consisted of about twenty-five head of cattle, a substitute for bread, made of the Maguay and other plants, berries, &c., and a large supply of beef on pack animals. He pursued the Indians, about fifteen in number, towards the Guadalupe's, as far as Escondido. This was undoubtedly the same party struck by the detachment of Kennedy's company on the 4th. Captain Lebo, in returning, scouted around the west side of the mountains, and arrived at the Fresno Carriso Mountains on the morning of the 7th, where he struck the trail of Victorio's whole force, considering it fortunate that the Indians who made the trail had not struck his company. He, however, followed the trail north, through Rattlesnake Cañon, until he come upon Captain Nolan's company, and soon after reported to me at Rattlesnake Springs.

Toward the evening Captain Livermore arrived with Company K, Eighth Cavalry, and a few Lipan scouts.

On the 8th, Lieutenant Pullman, with a detachment of the Eighth Cavalry, scouted through Rattlesnake Cañon, and followed the Indian trail some distance west into the mountains. In the afternoon Captain Baylor arrived with fifteen Texas rangers. The same evening, Captain Finley was sent with a detachment of Company C, Tenth Cavalry, to guard Apache Spring, twelve miles northwest, on the side of the mountains, where he picked up a horse and a few ponies, evidently strayed from the Indians.

On the 9th, with Captain Gilmore, Lieutenant Dodge, and Company H, Twenty-fourth Infantry, Lieutenant Read, Tenth Cavalry, Captain Livermore and his scouts, and the Pueblos, I climbed the rough and precipitous cliffs of the Sierra Diablo, two thousand feet high, and scouted over the mountains on foot as far as practicable. On the 10th, Company A, Tenth Cavalry, Company K, Eighth Cavalry, the Lipan scouts, the Texas rangers, Captain Nolan commanding, were ordered to scout south, through Rattlesnake Cañon, to the Fresno, and thence westward through the mountains, while, with Company C, Tenth Cavalry, I proceeded to Sulphur Springs, leaving Company H, Twenty-fourth Infantry, and Company K, Tenth Cavalry, Captain Gilmore commanding, at Rattlesnake Springs. Immediately upon arrival at Sulphur Springs, Companies H and G, Tenth Cavalry, under Captain Carpenter, were sent to scout around the west side of the mountains, while I remained with Companies C and G, Tenth Cavalry, at Sulphur Springs: Companies F and I, Tenth Cavalry, at the Guadalupe's, Captain Kennedy commanding, were directed to get in front of, and attack the Indians in case they succeeded in forcing their way northward.

The object of this disposition and movement of troops was to attack the Indians from all sides, if found in the mountains, or if they were forced out, to find the trail and pursue them. This caused Victorio and his band to move rapidly southward; the trail was found by Captains Nolan and Carpenter on the 11th, fifteen miles west of the Fresno. Captain Carpenter's horses being exhausted for want of water, he was obliged to leave the trail and proceed to Eagle Springs. Captain Nolan, however, with his command, followed the trail and pursued the Indians to the Rio Grande, twelve miles below Quitman, reaching there early on the 13th – Victorio, with the last of his band, having re-crossed into Mexico the evening before.

On the 13th, Company K, Tenth Cavalry, was ordered to Eagle Springs from Rattlesnake Cañon, and Company H, Twenty-fourth Infantry, joined me at Sulphur Springs, when, after arranging for supplies for the troops left at that point, I proceeded with that company and Shannon's train, *via* Prieto, thence opening a new road west of the Diablo and Carriso Mountains to Eagle Springs.

On the 18th, I sent Charles Berger, interpreter and scout, with the Lipans and Pueblos, on the trail of the Indians, into Mexico, to gain definite knowledge in regard to their whereabouts.

Company E, Tenth Cavalry, Captain Kelly commanding, was ordered to Fort Quitman to report to Captain Nolan, and Companies B, H, and K, Tenth Cavalry, under Captain Carpenter, to Ojo Caliente; Captain Livermore, with Company K, Eighth Cavalry, was ordered to Viejo Pass, and relieved from further duty in this district, to enable him to comply with his orders from department headquarters; Company I, Tenth Cavalry, was brought west from Viejo Pass to Eagle Springs.

Charles Berger and scouts returned from Mexico, after following the trail to the Candelaria Mountains. They found that the Indians were in a badly crippled condition, having their wounded with them, and their stock worn out, as an indication of which they were mostly on foot, driving their animals, avoiding their usual trails passing over and skirting the roughest broken country. The Mexican troops had neither attacked them nor gotten in their way, but had given them open passage westward, *via* Santa Maria River to Lake Guzman. This report has since been confirmed by General Buell, who states that his scouts report the Indians near that point with a camp of wounded.

If the Mexican troops had been ready and in condition to attack the Indians when they were forced across the Rio Grande, or if I had authority to pursue them into Mexico, thus giving them no time to rest, there is little doubt that Victorio and his band would have been captured or destroyed.

I left Eagle Springs on the 23rd of August for Fort Bliss, and arrived at that post on the 1st instant. The Mexican Government has certainly failed to take any decisive measures to expel Victorio and his band of marauders. The regular troops, who were moving from the south towards the Indians, were hastily withdrawn to Chihuahua on account of threatened revolution. There seems to be a tacit understanding between Victorio and many of the Mexicans, that so long as he does not make war upon them in earnest, he can take whatever food and other supplies he may need for his warriors. They know that he and his marauders belong to the United States, and think that our government should keep them at home and prevent them from raiding and invading their territory. It is probable that many claims for damages will be brought against the Unites States Government on account of depredations committees by Victorio and his band in Mexico. A large majority of the Mexicans oppose having our troops cross into their territory, and I do not think that the authority will be granted by the Mexican Government, as it would be very unpopular and might cause serious trouble. In any event, no effective co-operation need be expected, on account of the defective material and organization of the Mexican troops.

A force of Chihuahuan State troops, under command of Joaquin Terrassas, is being organized to move against the hostile Indians, but, to the present time, the Indian camp remains undisturbed in the vicinity of Lake Guzman.

I left Fort Bliss on the 4th instant, and arrived at Fort Concho on the 16th. While *en route* to this post, I arranged for the supply of all troops in the field up to October 31st, and, giving all necessary instructions, placed Major N.B. McLaughlen, Tenth Cavalry, in command of the troops in my absence.

During late operations, my command covered a belt of country fully fifty miles wide, from the Rio Grande to New Mexico, west of and beyond the limits of my district.

By the disposition made of my small force, and the genuine pluck and earnest activity of the troops, Victorio and his bold marauders were three times headed off; twice whipped; driven from their stronghold in the Sierra Diablo; and twice forced back into Mexico. The hurried manner in which they cut and torn the flesh from the dead and wounded animals, found in their camps and on their trails, indicates the food they were compelled to subsist on after their supplies were captured. The remains of several Indians lately killed, and fresh Indian graves, were found in the vicinity of their trails and late camps; and from unmistakable evidence, I am now confident that the Indians were much more severely handled during their short stay in Texas than I at first reported.

From the 28th of July, when they first crossed into Texas, until August 12th, when Victorio and the last of his badly demoralized band were the second time driven across the Rio Grande, their loss at the fights a Tenaja de los Palmas and Rattlesnake Cañon, and in the several skirmishes, was certainly thirty killed and wounded, very probably fifty, beside the loss of all their supplies, and from seventy-five to one hundred animals.

I am indebted to Capt. John C. Gilmore, Twenty-fourth Infantry, for the earnest and faultless manner in which he performed his duties.

First Lieut. W. H. Beck, Tenth Cavalry, A.D.C. and A.A.A.G., and Second Lieutenant Charles Dodge, jr., Twenty-fourth Infantry, A.A.Q.M. and A.C.S., discharged the important duties assigned them with promptitude and efficiency.

I am also pleased to acknowledge my indebtedness to Lieut. Col. J.E. Yard, Twenty-fourth Infantry, commanding officer Fort Davis, Texas, and to Lieut. S.L. Woodward, Tenth Cavalry, the energetic and efficient A.A.Q.M. and A.C.S. of that post, for their valuable aid in keeping transportation in good order, and forwarding supplies for the troops in the field.

Attention is invited to the enclosed tabular statement, showing movements made, and giving the names of all officers, companies, and detachments engaged, distances marched, &c.; and also to enclosed map, prepared by Sergt. Robert F. Joyce, under my direct supervision, which shows the routes taken, country scouted over, and embraces Western Texas and adjoining territory.

The great difficulties to be encountered in operating against Indians in Western Texas, throughout which there is great scarcity of water, cannot be conceived by any one unacquainted with the nature and extent of the country. Numerous and rugged and precipitous mountain ranges, broken by cañons, rise from the plains, while the foothills bordering the mountains, are cut into deep ravines and gullies, and the surface of the whole country is covered to a great extent, by immense Spanish bayonets, many varieties of cacti, and other thorny plants and entangling shrubs, affording hiding places every way suitable to aid the roaming savages in their predatory incursions.

Without the accurate knowledge of the country, which myself and troops have gained during three years hard work, scouting and exploring, we would not have been successful.

I trust that the services rendered by my command, during the late campaign, will meet with that recognition which earnest effort in the line of duty deserves.

Very respectfully, your obedient servant,

B.H. Grierson

Colonel Tenth Cavalry, Commanding

Appendix Two: Description of the Victorio Campaign by First Sergeant John F. Casey, Troop H, 10th Cavalry[1]

We arrived at Ft. Davis, Texas, May 1, 1875, from which Post I was on continuous scouting from ten days to thirty days, and from that to a year and half at a period. At this Post we were stationed ten years. From this Post we were continuously scouting either as a whole company or in detachments from ten to twelve men in each.

In the year 1879 and 1880, I was on another campaign which is known as the Victory [Victorio] Campaign, in pursuit of Muschalary [Mescalero] Indians which came from New Mexico to Texas, murdering and pillaging as they went, about four hundred strong. My company and several other troops, in fact a whole regiment, or parts of regiments were sent in pursuit of them. This campaign lasted about a year and four months. During this campaign we traced the Indians from Texas into Old Mexico and the Mexicans drove them back into Texas crossing the Rio Grande near El Paso, Texas. We first intercepted them at Eagle Springs, Texas, had a running fight about dark on the following day, and drove them back in toward Mexico and the Copoka [Capote] mountains and thence into the Crecey [?] mountains in the Salt Lake Valley where we

---

[1] This is the only firsthand account by an enlisted man that I have found. Most likely transcribed by someone other than Casey, it is recorded in Harold Sayre, *Warriors of Color* (Fort Davis: Harold Ray Sayre, 1995), pp. 108-109. The commanding officer of Company H, 10th Cavalry was Captain Louis Carpenter one of Grierson's most experienced and senior officers.

engaged in battle and drove them from the Salt Lake Valley into the mountains again, and two companies of us kept them engaged all day until about 3 o'clock in the afternoon when our ammunition ran out and we were called to the Reserves and other troops took our place in the firing line.[2] Shortly after the Indians retreated going in the direction of Old Mexico and between 4 and 5 o'clock in the evening my company was ordered to flank them on the west and keep them out of Old Mexico.

While traveling over an unknown trail over sage brush, sand and alkali we became very thirsty and very nearly perished from lack of water, as we had no fresh water, nothing but salty water for two days. About 7 o'clock that evening a cloud appeared in the horizon and in about twenty minutes the rain commenced pouring down in torrents which gave us fresh water for the first time in 24 hours. We got water and watered our stock and kept on the trail to Old Mexico. We arrived too late to keep the Indians off. We followed on the trail until we came to the Hot Springs in the bed of the Rio Grande, where the Indians had crossed into Old Mexico.[3] The Mexican soldiers who were on the opposite side, took up the trail and followed them into the Candleary Mountains, Mexico, and there captured all of the band except about eight, including Chief Victory, who was chief of the tribe. They beheaded him and carried his head to Mexico City. This ended the campaign.

---

[2] Rattlesnake Springs

[3] Carpenter and Captain Nicholas Nolan, Company A, 10th Cavalry, led the pursuit of Victorio south to the Rio Grande. As Grierson wrote in his *Report*, "the trail was found by Captains Nolan and Carpenter on the 11th fifteen miles west of the Fresno. Captain Carpenter's horses being exhausted for want of water, he was obliged to leave the trail and proceed to Eagle Springs. Captain Nolan, however, with his command, followed the trail and pursued the Indians to the Rio Grande."

Bibliography

Unpublished & Miscellaneous Documents and Sources:

Bryan, Kelly. Texas Naturalist. (Email and Interview).

Interpretative Handout on Civilian Employees. Fort Davis National Historic Site.

Levy, Benjamin. *Commanding Officer's Quarters, Fort Davis, Texas Furnishings Study.* Fort Davis National Historic Site.

Letter from the War Department to United States Congressman, R.E. Thomason, 1938, Referencing Lieutenant Frank Mills fight with Apache in Viejo Pass. Fort Davis National Historic Site File titled Viejo Pass.

Peppers, Hillary. Adult Services Librarian, Jacksonville Public Library, Jacksonville, Illinois. (Email).

Powell, Dr. Michael, Emeritus Professor of Biology and Director of the Herbarium, Sul Ross State University, Alpine, TX. (Email).

Roster of Soldiers Serving at Fort Davis, Fort Davis National Historic Site Data Base.

Sargent, Bernie. El Paso Historian. (Email).

Smith, Donna. *List of Physicians and Surgeons Serving at Fort Davis.* Unpublished Data Base. Fort Davis National Historic Site.

Utley, Robert. *Special Report on Fort Davis.* Santa Fe: National Park Service, 1960.

__________. *Utley's Scrapbook: Miscellaneous Documents Pertaining To Fort Davis.* Fort Davis National Historic Site.

Books:

Annual Report of the Secretary of War for the Year 1880, Volume I. Washington: Government Printing Office, 1880. (Google Books).

Agnew, Jeremy. *Life of a Soldier on the Western Frontier.* Missoula, Montana: Mountain Press Publishing Company, 2011.

Austerman, Wayne. *Sharps Rifles and Spanish Mules: The San Antonio – El Paso Mail, 1851-1881.* College Station: Texas A&M Press, 1985

Ball, Eve. *In the Days of Victorio: Recollections of a Warm Springs Apache.* Tucson: University of Arizona Press, 1970.

Bartlett, John Russell. *Personal Narrative of Explorations and Incidents in Texas, New Mexico, California, Sonora and Chihuahua, 1850-1853.* Vol. I. (Reprint) Chicago: Rio Grande Press, 1965.

Billington, Monroe Lee. *New Mexico's Buffalo Soldiers, 1866-1900.* Niwot: University of Colorado Press, 1991.

Bode, E.A. Edited by Thomas T. Smith. *A Dose of Frontier Soldiering: The Memoirs of Corporal E.A. Bode, Frontier Regular Infantry, 1877-1882.* Lincoln: University of Nebraska Press, 1994.

Borneman, Walter B. *Rival Rails: The Race to Build America's Greatest Transcontinental Railroad.* New York: Random House, 2010.

Brown, D. Alexander. *Grierson's Raid.* Urbana: University of Illinois Press, 1962.

Carroll, John M. (ed.). *The Black Military Experience in the American West.* New York: Liverright Press, 1971.

Chamberlain, Kathleen P. *Victorio: Apache Warrior and Chief.* Norman: University of Oklahoma Press, 2007.

Cozzens, Peter, (ed.). *The Army and the Indian: Eyewitnesses to the Indian Wars, 1865-1890.* Five Volumes. Mechanicsburg, PA: Stackpole Books, 2001-2005.

Dobak, William and Thomas Phillips. *The Black Regulars, 1866-1898.* Norman: University of Oklahoma Press, 2001.

Eggenhofer, Nick. *Wagons, Mules and Men: How the Frontier Moved West.* New York, Hastings House, 1961.

Ely, Glen Sample. *The Texas Frontier and the Butterfield Overland Mail, 1858-1861.* Norman: University of Oklahoma Press, 2016.

Emory, William H. *Notes of a Military Reconnoissance from Fort Leavenworth, in Missouri, to San Diego, in California Including Parts of the Arkansas, Del Norte, and Gila Rivers.* Washington, D.C.: Wendell and Van Benthuysen Printers, 1848.

Francell, Lawrence John. *Fort Lancaster: Texas Frontier Sentinel.* Austin: Texas State Historical Association, 1999.

Frazer, Robert. *Forts of the West.* Norman: University of Oklahoma Press, 1972.

Gillett, James B. *Six Years with the Texas Rangers.* New Haven: Yale University Press, 1963 reprint.

Girardi, Robert. *The Civil War Generals: Comrades, Peers, Rivals in Their Own Words.* Minneapolis: Zenith Press, 2013.

Glass, Major E.L.N. *The Tenth Cavalry.* Fort Collins, Old Army Press, 1972.

Goetzmann, William. *Army Exploration in the American West, 1803-1863*. New Haven: Yale University Press, 1959.

Grant, Ulysses S. *Personal Memoirs*. Edited by Caleb Carr. New York: Modern Library, 1999.

Green, Bill. *The Dancing Was Lively: Fort Concho, Texas a Social History,* San Angelo, TX: William Elton Green, 1974.

Groom, Winston. *Kearney's March: The Epic Creation of the American West, 1846-1847*. New York: Alfred A. Knopf, 2011.

Haley, J. Evetts. *Fort Concho and the Texas Frontier*. Midland, TX: West Texas Legacy Press, 2006.

Harris, Theodore (ed.). *The Memoirs of Henry O. Flipper*. Fort Worth: TCU Press. 1997.

Heitman, Francis B. *Historical Register and Dictionary of the United States Army, 1789-1903*. Vol. I.& II. Urbana: University of Illinois Press, 1965.

Hooker, Charles. *Confederate Military History*. (Vol. VII, Mississippi). Atlanta: Confederate Publishing Company, 1899.

Hutton, Paul Andrew. *Phil Sheridan and His Army*. Norman: University of Oklahoma Press, 1885.

Hutton, Paul Andrew and Durwood Ball. (eds, 2nd edition). *Soldiers West: Biographies from the Military Frontier*. Norman: University of Oklahoma Press, 2009.

Jacobson, Lucy and Mildred Nored. *Jeff Davis County, Texas*. Fort Davis: Fort Davis Historical Society, 1993.

Julyan, Robert. *The Place Names of New Mexico*. Albuquerque: University of New Mexico Press, 1988.

Kraft, Louis. *Gatewood and Geronimo*. Albuquerque: University of New Mexico Press, 2000.

Lalicki, Tom. *Grierson's Raid: A Daring Cavalry Strike through the Heart Of the Confederacy*. New York: Farrar, Straus, Giroux, 2004.

Leckie, Shirley Anne (editor). *The Colonel Lady on the Western Frontier: The Correspondence of Alice Kirk Grierson*. Lincoln: University of Nebraska Press, 1989.

Leckie, William. *The Buffalo Soldiers: A Narrative of the Negro Cavalry in The West*. Norman: University of Oklahoma Press, 1967.

Leckie, William and Shirley Leckie. *Unlikely Warriors: General Benjamin Grierson and his Family*. Norman: University of Oklahoma Press, 1984.

Lekson, Stephen. *Nana's Raid: Apache Warfare in Southern New Mexico, 1881.* El Paso: University of Texas at El Paso Press, 1987.

Leonard, Elizabeth. *Men of Color to Arms: Black Soldiers, Indian Wars, and The Quest for Equality.* New York: W.W. Norton & Company, 2010.

McChristian, Douglas (ed.). *Garrison Tangles in the Friendless Tenth: The Journal of First Lieutenant John Bigelow, Jr., Fort Davis, Texas.* Mattituck, New York, J.M. Carroll & Company, 1985.

__________. *Regular Army O! Soldiering on the Western Frontier, 1865-1891.* Norman: University of Oklahoma Press, 2017.

Miller, Darlis. *Soldiers and Settlers: Military Supply in the Southwest, 1861-1885.* Albuquerque: University of New Mexico Press, 1989.

Newcomb, W.W. *The Indians of Texas: From Prehistoric to Modern Times.* Austin: University of Texas Press, 1961.

Norris, L. David, James C. Mulligan and Odie B. Faulk. *William H. Emory:Soldier-Scientist.* Tucson: University of Arizona Press, 1998.

Phillips, Thomas. *Boots and Saddles: Military Leaders of the American West.* Caldwell, Idaho: Caxton Press, 2015.

Record of Engagements with Hostile Indians within the Military Department of the Missouri from 1868 to 1882. Compiled from Official Records, Lieutenant General Philip H. Sheridan, Commanding. Chicago: Headquarters Military Division of the Missouri, 1882.

Rickey, Don. *Forty Miles a Day on Beans and Hay.* Norman: University of Oklahoma Press, 1963.

Robinson, Charles H. *The Court Martial of Lieutenant Henry Flipper.* El Paso: University of Texas at El Paso Press, 1994.

__________. *The Men Who Wear the Star: The Story of the Texas Rangers.* New York: Random House 2000.

Sayre, Harold Ray. *Warriors of Color.* Fort Davis: Harold Ray Sayre, 1995.

Schubert, Frank N. *Black Valor: Buffalo Soldiers and the Medal of Honor, 1870-1898.* Wilmington, Delaware: Scholarly Resources, 1997.

__________.*Voices of the Buffalo Soldiers: Records, Reports, and Recollections of Military Life and Service in the West.* Albuquerque: University of New Mexico Press, 2003.

Smith, Sherry. *The View from Officers' Row, Army Perceptions of Western Indians.* Tucson: University of Arizona Press, 1990.

Smith, Thomas T. *The Old Army in Texas: A research Guide to the U.S. Army in Nineteenth Century Texas.* Austin: Texas State Historical Association, 2000.

Sonnichsen, C.L. *The Mescalero Apaches.* Norman: University of Oklahoma Press, 1973.

Stiles, T.J. *Custer's Trials: A Life on the Frontier of a New America.* New York: Alfred A. Knopf, 2015.

Stillman, J.D.B. *Wanderings in the Southwest in 1855.* Ed. Ron Tyler. Spokane, Washington: Arthur H. Clark Company, 1990.

Thain, Raphael. Edited by John M. Carroll. *Notes Illustrating the Military Geography of the United States, 1813-1880.* Austin: University of Texas Press, 1979.

Thrapp, Dan L. *The Conquest of Apacheria.* Norman: University of Oklahoma Press, 1967.

___________. *Encyclopedia of Frontier Biography.* 3 vols. Lincoln: University of Nebraska Press, 1988.

___________. *Victorio and the Mimbres Apaches.* Norman: University of Oklahoma Press, 1974.

Tyler, Ron, Editor in Chief. *Handbook of Texas.* Six Volumes. Austin: Texas State Historical Association, 1996.

Utley, Robert. *Frontier Regulars: The United States Army and the Indian, 1866-1891.* New York: Macmillan Publishing, 1973.

Wheelan, Joseph. *Bloody Spring: Forty Days that Sealed the Confederacy's Fate.* Boston: Da Capo Press, 2014.

___________. *Terrible Swift Sword: The Life of General Philip H. Sheridan.* Cambridge, MA: Da Capo Press, 2012.

White, Ronald C. *American Ulysses: A Life of Ulysses S. Grant.* New York: Random House, 2016.

Williams, Clayton W. *Texas' Last Frontier: Fort Stockton and the Trans-Pecos, 1861-1895.* College Station: Texas A&M Press, 1982.

Wooster, Robert. *Frontier Crossroads: Fort Davis and the West.* College Station: Texas A&M Press, 2006.

___________. *The Military and United States Indian Policy, 1865-1903.* New Haven: Yale University Press, 1888.

Articles & Pamphlets:

Roster of Non-Commissioned Officers of the Tenth U.S. Cavalry. St.
    Paul, Minnesota: Wm. Kennedy Printing Company, 1897.
    (Reprint, Bryan, Texas: J.M. Carroll & Company, 1983.)
Utley, Robert. *Fort Davis.* National Park Service Historical Handbook
    Series 38. Washington, 1965.
*Moving with the Frontier Army: Tenth Cavalry Officers' Wives Follow
    the Guidon.* Interpretative Handout, Fort Davis National Historic
    Site.

Index

Author Bio

Lawrence John Francell earned a Bachelor of Arts in History from Austin College and a Master of Arts in History from the University of Texas at Austin. He has worked for Texas Parks & Wildlife, and the National Park Service at Fort Davis National Historic Site. He spent many years in the museum business and was a partner in FAE Worldwide, an international museum and arts services company. In 1996 he sold his portion of the business to move to Fort Davis where he and his wife Beth purchased and restored her family home.

He has spent over twenty years in county government, and is the author of *Fort Lancaster: Texas Frontier Sentinel*; *Planning for the Move of a Museum Collection*; *How Indian Emily Saved Fort Davis*; *What's in a Name: Why Fort Davis Was Named for Jefferson Davis and Why the Name Was Never Changed*; *Amid Shot and Shell of a Hundred Battlefields: The Life of Samuel Percival Greene*, plus numerous articles on local history and museum operations.

One of his personal goals is the recognition and preservation of the original and unimproved portion of the Davis Mountains State Park Highway, the subject of his book *The Scenic Loop: Davis Mountains State Park Highway.*

Several of Larry's books can be found in Fort Davis and Alpine area bookstores and gift shops, as well as for purchase online.

www.ingramcontent.com/pod-product-compliance
Lightning Source LLC
Chambersburg PA
CBHW060448310726
48977CB00001B/365